DO NOT REMOVE
CARDS FROM POCKET

ALLEN COUNTY PUBLIC LIBRARY

FORT WAYNE, INDIANA 46802

You may return this book to any agency, branch,
or bookmobile of the Allen County Public Library.

DEMCO

COLLEGE
GETTING IN
AND
STAYING IN

D. Bruce Lockerbie and Donald R. Fonseca

WILLIAM B. EERDMANS PUBLISHING COMPANY
GRAND RAPIDS, MICHIGAN

Copyright © 1990 by Wm. B. Eerdmans Publishing Co.
255 Jefferson Ave. S.E., Grand Rapids, Mich. 49503

Printed in the United States of America

Library of Congress Cataloging-in-Publication Data

Lockerbie, D. Bruce
  College: getting in and staying in / D. Bruce Lockerbie and
Donald R. Fonseca.
       p.   cm.
  ISBN 0-8028-0424-1
  1. College Student orientation—United States.   I. Fonseca, Donald R.,
1932–   . II. Title.
LB2343.32.L63   1990
378.1'98—dc20

90-32755
CIP

To our children

Don, Kevin, and Ellyn
Cindy, Sandy, and Diane

whose college experience makes this book real

Contents

Introduction

Your high-school years are finally coming to an end. In a year or two, you'll be caught up in the rituals of graduation. There'll be award ceremonies to attend, yearbooks to autograph, parties to enjoy. Then the big day itself will arrive, and you and your classmates will be marching in cap and gown to Sir Edward Elgar's "Pomp and Circumstance." The ceremony will include speeches by the valedictorian and the salutatorian. In between those speeches the principal or superintendent, assisted by the president of the school board, will distribute the diplomas.

All in all, this is a joyous occasion. But then why do so many teenagers feel such anxiety as they face the close of their high-school years?

Because they're saying good-bye—not only to friends but to a very special chapter in their lives. Because they're leaving behind the relatively carefree experiences of childhood and early adolescence for the new responsibilities of becoming adults.

And for thousands of teenagers, going to college represents another step toward young adulthood and the full freedoms and responsibilities of being self-reliant and, eventually, self-sufficient. It's a definite step in the direction of final emancipation from their parents' home and obligation to support them. And that can be kind of scary. It's true that some high-school students are already well on the way toward that kind of freedom, while others aren't—but that really doesn't matter. Going to college is stressful for everyone because it represents *change*.

Most of us claim that we hate anything old-fashioned, that we prefer whatever's new. But the fact is that change often frightens us as much as it may fascinate us. In the face of change, we're troubled by self-doubt: "Will I fit in? Will people like me? Will I succeed?"

Questions like these are perfectly normal. If you're feeling and expressing these doubts, remember that you're not alone, and that it's okay for you to wonder in this way, to question your own self-confidence, just as long as you understand that the real questions you're asking are these: "Am I ready to accept change in my life? Am I ready for change now?" Of course, we all recognize that change is inevitable, but some change can be postponed until we're ready for it.

The authors of this book are very familiar with these feelings. Together, we've seen our six children—Don, Kevin, and Ellyn Lockerbie; Cindy, Sandy, and Diane Fonseca—walk across the high-school stage with diploma in hand. But long before those happy moments, we endured the anxieties and questions many families—teens and parents together—face. Is college the next logical step, or should some other alternative be considered? If college is the next step, where should our daughter apply? If our son is accepted at more than one college, where should he enroll? How do we pay for a college education and make it the best experience possible?

We know all this not just because of our experiences with our own children. It's also our job to know: we're teachers and administrators at The Stony Brook School, a college-preparatory school located on Long Island, east of New York City.

Together we've taught and coached and led choirs and prepared debaters and counseled students for a combined total of more than sixty years. In that time we've worked to prepare thousands of students and their parents for college admission; we've served on commissions and committees of the College Board and its testing agent, Educational Testing Service; and we've also assisted other schools and colleges as consultants throughout this continent and around the world.

Most important, we know that every teenager and every family is unique. Situations may be similar, and certain problems may be common to all, but the individuals involved are special and deserve special care. So the advice we give in this book is based on general principles that we believe can be applied to your specific circumstances. And we've designed many sections of the book so that they'll function as personal checklists you can use as you make various decisions about college.

"Getting in and staying in" is what we wish for you, and we hope this book will help you do just that.

D. Bruce Lockerbie
Donald R. Fonseca
Stony Brook, New York

CHAPTER 1

It Isn't Automatic

Let's face it: College isn't for everyone—at least not right away, and certainly not immediately following high school. And not necessarily for four years in a row.

A report from the National Center for Education Statistics shows this graph of college entrance in the last decade:

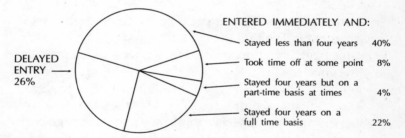

You'll notice that, of all high-school graduates who do go on to college, slightly more than one-quarter (26%) delay entering college for some reason. Of the 74 percent who go directly to college from high school, more than half stay less than four years; another group takes time off, and yet another continues only on a part-time basis.

Only 22 percent of the entire college population attend four years on a full-time basis.

1

STRAIGHT AS AN ARROW

Of course, there are lots of reasons for going to college and for choosing to go right out of high school. Some are very noble:

- to advance your education and preparation for your intended life's work;
- to avoid any possible sidetracking from your intended life's work caused by the temporary thrill of making money on a job;
- to fulfill your hunger and thirst for knowledge.

Do any of these sound like your reasons? Other reasons seem more practical than noble:

- to maintain the momentum of regular school attendance;
- to build immediately on what you've learned in high school;
- to stay in sync with your peers in the same age bracket so you don't fall behind in the race for a job;
- to insure that you're qualified for a good job that provides "the good life."

Some students are afraid to step out of the groove (or rut!) of going to school because they think they might never go back. Others are afraid they'll forget everything they ever learned in school if they don't keep the great snowball of information rolling. Still others are afraid that the rest of the world will get too big a jump on them if they don't keep up the tempo and go straight off to college.

Every one of these fears may be valid for somebody, but are any of them valid for you?

Other reasons for going directly to college are almost too realistic and honest to put into words. Some students might even be a trifle embarrassed to admit they've had such thoughts, the most unspeakable of which is this:

- I'm going to college to pass the time while I figure out what else to do with my life.

That's getting right down to the core, isn't it? Since some students don't know what they'll do tomorrow—never mind the next four years—they decide, "Hey, I'll go to college!" This is fine if their parents are fantastically wealthy and a bill for twelve grand and up per year would be no problem. But for most parents, paying for college tuition and room and board while their teenager "finds himself" would seem like a huge waste of money.

A LEGITIMATE HOLDING ACTION

At the same time, we understand that lots of responsible teenagers don't know what they want to do in the next ten minutes—and you may be one of them. So how can you possibly plan what to do with the rest of your life? You don't have an "intended life's work" or any real sense of calling to one profession or another. For you, a four-year tour through Wonderland (also known as "a liberal arts education") may be precisely what the doctor ordered as a way of introducing you to the vast and varied future possibilities awaiting.

By studying a broad range of subjects first instead of limiting yourself to some particular technical training—to become a civil engineer, say, or a forest ranger—and then following up with some specialized instruction after college, you're more likely to discover the one area of knowledge that most fascinates you, an area of knowledge to which you can commit the next thirty or forty years of your life.

In other words, that's one of the legitimate experiences a college education should provide: a holding action that gives you the chance to learn what life's opportunities and options are and where you best fit among them. Assuming you do decide to go to college, you shouldn't feel embarrassed if, a few weeks after your high-school graduation, you *still* haven't made up your mind about what you'll study and prepare to be.

ANSWERING THE PRIMARY QUESTION

Why does anyone decide to go to college? Let's look at those reasons again—noble, practical, or otherwise. Some people are compelled simply by the quest, the hunger for knowledge. These are the people our society depends on to think the profound thoughts and write the influential books and eventually make the scientific discoveries that will cure cancer and do other wonderful things.

If you're one of these people, congratulations! We need you and your good mind at work. For you, the formal discipline of a college/university education—undergraduate, graduate, and probably post-graduate—will be a long haul, with plenty of barriers in the way to discourage you. But, as one slogan puts it, "a mind is a terrible thing to waste," so don't put it off without good reason.

One nice advantage for a student like you is that a college education is usually free. With SAT or ACT scores in the stratospheric range, you're probably the very sort of person who attracts scholarship opportunities that will pay every bill from now until you get your Ph.D.

One of our daughters has followed that route. When she got her high-school diploma, she didn't have any strong sense of direction pointing her toward a doctorate in French and a career in teaching. In fact, after high school, she spent a year in Scotland as an exchange student at a British boarding school for girls, all expenses paid. That was especially nice for her parents because it gave them an extra year to get ready for college bills. But then she earned an athletic grant in track, and her four years of college were paid for, with extra supplements from academic scholarships. Following college she spent a year in Switzerland to polish her French major, then earned a master's degree in French, and finally went on to get a doctorate—all paid for by her university's fund to support graduate students by what's called a teaching fellowship.

If you can get this kind of financial support, fine—but remember, go after it only if you're committed to working hard as a student and to using what you learn to make a difference in the world.

Others go to college for reasons besides intellectual curiosity; it's a ticket to a better life. Such people don't take education lightly, and they don't take it for granted. We've seen students overseas—in Africa, in Asia—for whom the chance to go to college or a university is literally a one-in-a-million opportunity. In some countries—Bangladesh, for example, where less than 25 percent of the population can read and write—people cherish their ability to read and write as a mark of honor. Some citizens actually wear glasses as a status symbol, a sign that they're literate!

In fact, in Bangladesh it's not unusual to see a sign outside someone's home or place of business that reads "B.A. Fail." This means that the person attempted to complete the university course of study but was unsuccessful. Yet he's so proud of having gotten that far, even though he failed the final exams for his degree, that he hangs a shingle announcing his academic standing to the world.

We don't have quite that same intensity about education in North America. In fact, our society tends to take going to college for granted because higher education is now considered a *right* rather than a *privilege*. The authors of this book don't happen to agree that every human being *deserves* a college education; we still believe that an individual appreciates most what he or she works hard to earn. So it's possible that you don't actually know anybody quite so worked up about going to college as someone in Bangladesh might be. But, believe us, there are families all over the world, as well as here in the United States and Canada, scrimping and saving to be able to send their most promising daughters and sons to college—and they'll be the first-ever in their families to achieve that rank.

As we've already said, another sound reason for going to college is to prepare for your life's work, if you already know what that's going to be. You may be one of the many teenagers who know what they want to do with their lives and who are eager to start their necessary preparation. You've looked down the road and seen four years of undergraduate and six years of graduate studies, plus years of apprenticeship or internship. Why postpone the inevitable? Let's get started, you say. To us, that makes good sense, provided you're motivated toward a specific career by your own ambition rather than forced toward it by somebody else's expectations of you.

Every year we meet young men and women bent under a double emotional burden. It's bad enough to be seventeen and supposedly competing with every other high-school junior or senior who wants a good education; it's even worse when you find that you're also competing against your own mom or dad. Maybe your mom was homecoming queen and president of her sorority at the state university, and she desperately wants her daughter to win the same prizes. Maybe your dad was strictly Ivy League and what they called a "big man on campus," so it's simply assumed that you, his son, will follow in his footsteps.

But what if the cheerleader's daughter doesn't have her mother's social interests? What if the Ivy Leaguer's son prefers tearing apart a car engine and putting it back together? Is it so awful for a son to have his own interests and goals? Is it odd that a daughter's ambitions should differ from her parents' high hopes for her?

DELAYING ENTRY TO COLLEGE

Attending college isn't the automatic next step for some people. Maybe you're one for whom it isn't the best next step in your life—perhaps someday but not now; maybe not ever. Whatever your choice, that fact shouldn't cause a fracture in your own self-respect or in the love that you and other family members feel for each other.

There are many reasons for delaying entry to college:

You may feel that you need a break from the rigors of going to school.

After all, you've been riding the school bus since you were a five-year-old in kindergarten; you've been hitting the books almost every night since sixth grade; you've been writing term papers and book reports for what seems like forever. Your brain has been sizzled by a line of rationalization that goes like this.

- "The more you study, the more you know; the more you know, the more you forget; the more you forget, the less you know. So why study?"

If this is the way you feel, it's time for recess from school. So going to college gets put on hold, at least for the present.

You may have no real idea of the purpose in going to college or why going to college could benefit you now or later in life.

Some people treat their education as if they were guinea pigs on a treadmill: they just keep on scrambling because others seem to be doing the same thing. They have no sense of direction, except that somebody has handed them a college catalog, and so they suppose that the next destination after high school must be a college campus somewhere. But they're not sure why. What's college for? Is it a place of training? of preparation for a career or profession? Is it necessary for acquiring technical skills? mandatory for obtaining credentials? essential to a broadening of knowledge and understanding? Some of these? All of the above? Rather than stumble into college for no reason or the wrong reason, you might prefer to investigate the purpose of college before committing yourself and a hefty wad of the family fortune on finding-out-as-you-go.

You may be one of the few people who possess such a rare gift for inventing gadgets or composing music or selling real estate or playing basketball that going to college is really a detour from your main highway to success.

We know a composer whose music underscores some of the top movies and TV shows. He learned his art by playing and writing music, not by going to college. We know a major TV producer who flunked out of two colleges after only a semester in each. We know the world's leading salesman for one of the largest corporations; he's barely a high school graduate, yet he appears to be enormously successful at what he does. As a high-school player from Petersburg, Virginia, the all-star basketball center Moses Malone went straight to the pros.

But these people are one-in-a-million. Most of us lack the genius to make it at world-class level from the ranks of high school. Most of us need whatever maturing a college environment provides. Eventually, you too may find that missing out on a college education has been a handicap rather than an advantage. If you do, you'll be eager to make up for lost time.

You may need to work for a year or more to acquire the funds necessary to pay for a college education.

The costs of a college education are more than most families can afford, without taking out a loan or a second mortgage on the house. Every dime the student can contribute helps. But if you haven't earned much during your high-school years or haven't had a summer job that paid you well enough to allow you to save for your college expenses, you may not have much of a bank account to offer as your share of the costs. An alternative to putting your family more deeply in debt might be for you to take a year or so between high-school graduation and college entrance to make some money for college.

It won't be easy. Jobs of any kind may be scarce in your community. Even when you get hired, most jobs for which you qualify won't pay more than the current minimum wage. You'll have expenses and payroll deductions that will reduce your earnings; you'll also have to discipline yourself to save for your college goal. But one thing's for certain: You'll probably appreciate your college education more than the classmate who's coasting on somebody else's finances because you'll know how much it cost you to get there.

To get started with your higher education, you may need to work full-time or part-time while you attend a local community college as a part-time student.

In most states, a system of public two-year colleges has been developed under the auspices and control of the state university. They used to be called "junior colleges" and in some cases still are; now the preferred term for these public institutions is "community colleges." These colleges are funded partly by the state and partly by the county in which they're located and whose name they bear: Suffolk County Community College in Selden, New York, or Beaufort County Community College in

Washington, North Carolina. Few of these colleges provide housing, expecting their students to commute. As a result, tuition and fees are extraordinarily modest.

Because your state's Department of Higher Education stands behind the quality of instruction given in its community colleges, credit earned for passing courses at a community college will be transferrable to a public four-year college in the same state. This means that, upon acquiring four semesters' worth of credits, you can usually enter a public university in your state as a junior.

Furthermore, in many states, when you've decided to enroll in a four-year public college, you may find that you're shown preference over other transfer students. For instance, in our area, students completing four semesters (with a 2.5 average) at Suffolk County Community College on Long Island are automatically admitted as juniors by the State University of New York at Stony Brook.

However, if you wish to enroll in a private college or university, you may find that fewer of your community college credits are readily transferred; you may also discover that admission as a transfer student is competitive rather than automatic.

You may know yourself well enough to realize that you're not ready to go away to college just yet.

A young lady we admire named Karen went off eagerly to a college in another state. Unfortunately, she was placed in off-campus housing, in an apartment she shared with other women, out of the mainstream of college life. She wasn't ready for that kind of college experience and was miserable throughout her first semester. At Christmas, she told friends, "If I don't get a change in housing, I don't know what I'm going to do." When no relief in her housing situation could be found, she and her parents made a wise decision under those circumstances: she withdrew from that college and reapplied to one of the other colleges that had accepted her application when she was a high-school senior. She won't be going there until next September, but in the meantime she's working and attending a nearby community college to keep her credits current. And frankly, she's enjoying being at home for just a little longer.

If any of these reasons for delaying college entrance is yours, more power to you. Such delays can be very constructive.

LEARNING NEVER ENDS

Whatever alternative you choose instead of going to college directly from high school, be assured that your education—yes, even your *compulsory* education—hasn't ended. Whether you become a salesman or a bank teller, a clerk in a department store or a security guard, almost any employer will require you to take courses in the particular methods and techniques required to do that job well. As new machines come along, you'll need formal training to learn how to use them; as new regulations are passed, you'll have to take tests to prove that you know, understand, and can apply these regulations to your work.

There's no way around it: You'll be going to school long after you thought you'd tossed away your last textbook.

So, if you've found a good enough reason to go to college *now,* if you're convinced that it's the right decision for you at this precise time in your life, read on. If not, maybe a frank talk with your parents, your school counselor, and/or your pastor is the best idea.

SOLVING THE ADMISSIONS PUZZLE

Of course, even if you're determined to go on to college directly from high school, getting into the college of your first choice may not be a simple matter. You have to realize that the whole business of college admissions is pretty much of a mystery, even to those of us whose job it is to know about such things. Here's why.

For some time, statistics have been indicating a major drop in the number of eighteen-year-olds: 3.6 million in 1986, down to 3.2 million in 1994. This represents a decline of 17 percent from the previous low in 1968. You'd think that this would leave a far smaller number of potential college students, and that a smaller pool of prospective candidates would mean that colleges and universities ought to be begging for students. Which would seem to indicate that you could easily get into any college you could pay for.

Wrong! It so happens that the most selective colleges—and even some of the less selective ones—have been experiencing the greatest boom in their numbers of applicants in many years. Recently, Kenyon College in Ohio zoomed to 2,450 applications for only 410 places in the freshman class; Connecticut College in New London received 3,223 applications for 475 freshman openings; Colby College in Maine had over 3,500 applications for about 400 places.

What might explain this? In some cases, colleges are doing a better job of marketing themselves in distant parts of the country, using videotapes and broader mailings to attract interest in places where they hadn't bothered to promote themselves in the past. In other cases, students are applying to a greater number of colleges, protecting themselves from striking out by applying to several more colleges than the one or two at the top of their lists. For instance, an admissions officer at Middlebury College in Vermont reports that, on the average, applicants to his college had also applied to four others.

With these increased numbers has also come increased competition. For instance, at Pomona College in Claremont, California, some 45 percent of the freshman class scored over 700 out of 800 on the SAT math section. A nationwide survey by *College Bound*, a newsletter for college-admissions personnel and school counselors, reports that 54 percent of the colleges responding indicated receiving higher test scores from current applicants than from applicants in previous years.

At the same time, the number of applicants being disappointed by rejection is also increasing. The *New York Times* reported on one such case. A senior at the very tough Bronx High School of Science who had a 93 grade average, SAT scores of 1490, and perfect attendance applied to Harvard, Yale, Stanford, Cornell, and Pennsylvania. Results? Waiting list at Penn, rejection at all others.

Why he rang up a near zero is anybody's guess, but a few hints might help you put your own status as an applicant in better perspective.

1. The more selective the college, the stiffer the competition.

Recently, more than half the freshmen at Wheaton College in Illinois were either valedictorians or salutatorians in their high-school graduating classes. This doesn't leave much room for those with more average class standing.

2. Colleges aren't interested in one-dimensional people.

We have no way of knowing for sure, but it's possible that the bright student in the admissions illustration was too wrapped up in his studies. All brains, no heart—or, perhaps, no body. No interest in anything outside the physics lab; no record of belonging to the school choir or writing for the school newspaper or running on the cross-country team or managing the chess club. Even a genius stands a good chance of rejection if all he can show is a one-track mind for scholarly pursuits. Colleges know that such people burn themselves out—and may take a few others down in flames with them.

3. Colleges use various point systems and scales to rank their applicants according to achievement.

Few colleges are willing to explain just how they arrive at these rankings, but we know they use a point-scale to weigh and counterbalance activities against academic scores. For instance, membership on the debate squad may be worth one point; success at the regional or state-wide level may earn up to five points; but experience in national forensic competition could be worth up to ten points. So the higher you go in your competition or activity, the more favorably a college views your application.

4. Colleges look for applicants with specific skills and talents to add to those of undergraduates or replace those of graduating seniors.

Every college athlete runs out of playing time after four or five years and must be replaced by a freshman or a sophomore. The same thing happens with French horn players and actors and photographers and poets. As college classes come and go, graduating artists must be replaced by new arrivals. If you have a particular talent, hone it well and keep it sharp. There's a college out there in need of a tuba player or a theatrical set designer or someone who can run a soundboard or who can speak well.

5. Colleges take into consideration the reputed quality of individual high schools and their standing with either state or regional accrediting associations.

Sad to say, not all English teachers are as challenging and inspiring as yours; not all dramatic productions of *The Music Man* are of the same high quality as yours; not all schools or states have the same high standards as yours. However, it's also true that some schools are even more demanding than yours. Colleges tend to know which are the most high-powered schools, which schools consistently produce graduates with keen minds and broad abilities in the arts and athletics. So if an admissions officer has to choose between two applicants with similar academic records and a list of comparable activities, he or she will almost always choose the applicant from the school with the better reputation for turning out capable people.

6. Colleges want and need a certain measure of ethnic, racial, gender, and geographical diversity.

Every college designs its own "profile" for an ideal entering class: so many scholars, so many political activists, so many artists, so many athletes, so many world-travelers, so many average students. Most colleges won't admit to having quotas of any sort, but all of them do. For instance, state universities must admit a higher number of in-state applicants than out-of-state candidates. That's why it's so hard for someone from Maine to gain admission to Chapel Hill or University of Virginia; that's why a Hoosier struggles to get admitted to UCLA or Cal-Berkeley. In much the same way, coed institutions will determine what ratio of male-to-female students best suits their accommodations and their image. Under the Affirmative Action/Equal Opportunity regulations, any college receiving federal funds must be able to show that it's providing ample room for minority candidates. For these kinds of reasons, the colleges to which you apply will be looking to see how your application fits the profile they've designed for next year's freshman class.

Those are some of the realities of the college admissions game.

Are you prepared to play?

CHAPTER 2

The Hallowed Halls of Ivy

Many college graduates tend to get romantic, even teary-eyed about their college days. And why not? For the most part, those college years are full of pleasant memories—practical jokes and parties with roommates, sports victories and sometimes academic victories, deep and lasting friendships, perhaps even a serious romance and courtship leading to marriage.

Much of your initial thinking about college may be just as rose-colored and unrealistic as the memories of middle-aged alumni at a class reunion. But as you become better informed about the realities of college life—the sort of things alumni don't often talk about—you'll make wiser decisions based on that information.

Most high-school juniors and seniors get their first—maybe their only—impressions of college life from some sort of hero worship of a teacher, coach, youth pastor, older sibling, or other admired figure—a famous athlete, for instance—who attended a certain college. As a result of this admiration, early loyalties develop.

Don Lockerbie wore a Duke sweatshirt for years when he was in high school just because he admired an Olympic runner from Duke. Did he go to that fine university? No. Ironically, he wound up choosing the University of North Carolina at

Chapel Hill, Duke's greatest rival, and then both competed and coached against the neighboring Blue Devils.

Other teenagers learn about particular colleges by watching football games on TV. They see the huge stadium filled with excited, supportive fans; they see the glamorous cheerleaders forming their pyramid and drawing roars of approval from the crowd; they see the famous players, who seem invincible and bigger than life. It's all spectacular and exciting.

But that's not exactly what college is all about. There's another view of college life that too many high-school students miss. At halftime of those same broadcasts, while the high-school junior is away from the TV screen—probably checking out the contents of the refrigerator—what he may not see is the thirty-second promotional clip the networks allow each university.

All these quick trips to Notre Dame or Nebraska or Southern Cal are alike. They show libraries and research labs, not the athletic fields; they show Nobel prize-winning professors, not coaches; they show earnest students, not full-time athletes. As a matter of fact, if you believed the commercials, you'd think that universities exist for only those students with the highest IQ's and SAT scores; you'd also suppose that football is only a minor entertainment instead of the single greatest source of revenue for those institutions.

Another source of information about college is an older brother or sister or an older friend, someone already enrolled in college and home for the summer. Sometimes you have to take what they tell you with a grain of salt. Very few college students come home at Thanksgiving just bursting to describe the thrill of writing a research paper or fulfilling a lab requirement or learning to speak Spanish. They prefer to talk about the fraternity party or dorm picnic or weekend at the beach or the awful food or the boring professors or the all-nighters they pulled to get a minimal passing grade or the time they stole the other college's mascot or the great football victory over the archrivals from a neighboring campus.

College life includes some of both—the social as well as the academic, the parties as well as the pressure. That's why we've decided to include this chapter early in the book. In a way, it's like the previous chapter—a deliberate dose of reality to counter some more of your fantasies about going to college, just to help you be prepared.

LEAVING FANTASYLAND BEHIND

The college experience is a rude shock to teenagers who aren't expecting some of the ups and downs that naturally occur whenever large groups of strangers form a new community. And every student, even those at a smaller college where most students know each other by name—indeed, even at a Christian college where everyone professes to be a believer in Jesus Christ—encounters times of loneliness and discouragement. Knowing this in advance won't spare you from feeling blue occasionally, but it may help you prepare for the emotional roller coaster that afflicts many college students.

Let's get specific. Among other things, going to college means

- managing your own time and money and diet and laundry;
- planning ahead to complete assignments;
- learning how to survive on too little sleep;
- developing positive relationships with other people, despite differences in speech and custom, race or religion;
- negotiating and bargaining with others to reach amiable compromises;
- giving up, in most instances, the privilege of having your own private room and living in it pretty much as you please;
- spending some lonely days and nights waiting out a stuffy

nose or a case of flu or a sprained ankle without Mom there to act as nurse;

- enduring hectic hours and *pressure/pressure/pressure.*

College means *change* and *challenge.* Are you ready for a few changes? Are you up to a few challenges?

To find out if you're ready for "the hallowed halls of ivy," try answering some pointed questions about a variety of topics you may or may not have thought about before. Your parents may want to add some observations of their own.

1. How attached are you to the comforts of home?

- How many nights have you slept on a cot in a summer-camp cabin?
- How much do you cherish your privacy in the bathroom?
- If your house happens to have air conditioning and a quiet heating system, how adaptable are you to window fans and clanking radiators in an old dormitory building?
- How accustomed are you to something other than the comforts of home?
- Have you ever experienced, faced up to, and overcome a bout of homesickness?

If your answers to these questions suggest that you're pretty much of a homebody, you should realize what you may have to adjust to at college—a dorm room and a totally unfamiliar world of peeling paint and lumpy mattresses, open toilets and showers, too much or too little heat, and other surprises of communal living.

2. How much do you know about cooking and eating right?

- How resourceful are you in the kitchen?
- Can you make a sandwich? Can you boil water for a cup of instant coffee?
- Do you know how a microwave oven operates?
- Have you discovered the importance of washing—not just rinsing—dishes and utensils?
- Do you know anything about nutrition?
- Do you understand why some products—particularly snack foods like potato chips and other crunchy items— aren't really *foods* at all?
- Do you know how to eat healthy foods and avoid junk?
- Do you keep regular eating habits, or do you overeat, then fast?
- Do you know about anorexia nervosa and bulimia?

Your answers to these questions will help you determine if you could manage to make your own meals if you lived off campus in a house or apartment. They'll also help you figure out if you're a healthy eater—able to choose nutritious foods from the often strange assortment provided by the college food service—or a foolish eater.

3. Please don't be insulted, but how adept are you at managing your own personal hygiene, the cleanliness of your living quarters and your clothing?

- Do you bathe daily without being reminded by someone else?
- Has anyone ever handed you a bottle of Scope?
- How often do you change your underwear?
- How many mornings a week do you make your bed?

- Have you ever done household chores like vacuuming and dusting?
- Who's responsible for the garbage collection at your house?
- Have you learned how to operate a washing machine and a clothes dryer?
- Can you keep your socks in pairs?
- Can you thread a needle and sew on a button or mend a hem?
- Have you ever ironed a pair of slacks without scorching them?
- Can you change the sheets on a bed?

The point of these questions is to test how much real responsibility you've taken or been given for your own hygiene and housekeeping. In college you'll be responsible for basic maintenance of yourself and (in most cases) your living quarters.

4. How much responsibility have you assumed for your own finances?

- Do your parents still dole out a weekly allowance, or do you earn your own spending money?
- Do you carry your cash with you or leave it on your desk or in your dresser drawer?
- Do you have both a savings account and a checking account?
- Can you balance your checkbook?
- Has your account ever been overdrawn?
- Have you used an automated bank machine?
- Have you been given or have you tried to get a bank card or a credit card? Do you know the difference between these two forms of plastic money?
- Do you know the meaning and importance of your personal credit rating?

- Do you frequently borrow money from your brother or sister? Are you an easy mark for somebody who wants to borrow money?
- Have you ever been stuck with little or no cash and no way of getting any soon?
- Other than pleading for help from your parents, would you know what to do in a real financial emergency?

As we'll discuss later, money problems in all forms are one of the most common difficulties that college students face. Everything costs more than you and your parents expected. Everybody else seems to have money to burn. It's tough to stay in the dorm room when everyone else is going out for a late snack; it's tougher still to explain why you can't share the cost of a pizza party. Sometimes the money problem isn't a shortage but the mismanaging of whatever money you had—maybe you spent a month's worth of cash in a single weekend. To keep money in your pocket, you need to be thrifty and use your common sense.

5. Have you ever shared your room with anyone?

- Are you prepared to live with someone else's odd preferences and behavior?
- What if your roommate likes to keep your room cold in the middle of winter?
- Suppose your roommate enjoys listening to Bach and Beethoven at high volume, while your preference tends more toward Willie Nelson or the latest band?
- What if your roommate, unlike you, isn't accustomed to taking a daily bath?
- What if your roommate snores?
- What if your roommate is a heavy cigarette smoker?
- What if your roommate is a heavy drinker, perhaps even an alcoholic?

- What if your roommate turns out to be a drug user or dealer?
- What if your dorm turns out to be the campus crack-house?
- What if your roommate invites someone to spend the night to have sex in your room? Will you stay in the room or leave for their convenience—or will you tell them to go somewhere else?
- What if you discover that your roommate is homosexual or bi-sexual?
- What if your roommate starts talking about suicide?
- What if your roommate objects to your devotional habits—say, to your praying and reading your Bible?
- Will you invite your roommate to go with you to a local church on Sundays?
- What if your roommate is an ardent Christian of a denomination other than yours and is constantly trying to persuade you that your church is in error?
- What if your roommate invites you to attend the campus meeting of Inter-Varsity Christian Fellowship or Campus Crusade for Christ or Fellowship of Christian Athletes? Will you be ashamed to be seen at those Christian gatherings?

Obviously, these questions aim at testing some of the realities of living with a total stranger under the most intimate conditions—as roommates in a college dorm. Some colleges ask several compatability questions on their dorm applications, but many colleges don't. So you have to be prepared to share living space with someone quite unlike yourself—but also to know when you're just too different to make it work.

Take Don's experience. As a freshman, Don had a roommate who was a science fanatic. He'd wake up at 2:00 a.m. with an inspiration and work on his physics problems out loud and with the lights blazing. As a senior, Don got paired with a homosexual drummer for a rock band. Kevin was paired with a sloppy roommate with such bad habits (like never shower-ing) that Kevin eventually kicked him out. And Ellyn found herself with an aspiring fashion model who had so many clothes that they would have taken up all the closet space if Ellyn hadn't staked out a little space for her own stuff.

Granted, some of these situations are atypical, and you wouldn't necessarily find yourself in any of them. Still, it's worthwhile to think about how you would react if you had to face one of these challenges.

6. Are you prepared for a variety of social situations that may lead to intense romantic relationships and even to marriage?

- Have you done much dating during high school?
- Are you currently involved in a high-school romance?
- Are you promising or are you expected to promise that you'll be true to that high-school love, no matter how many miles separate you? Do you have any idea how unrealistic that promise may become?
- Beyond your parents' early talk about "the birds and bees," have you been instructed clinically about your sex-uality and sexual functions? Do you know how your body works?
- Have you developed your own standards of sexual moral-ity? Are you aware of how few of your peers might share those same standards?
- Have you ever been propositioned by a stranger, asked to have sex just for the physical thrill of it? If not, do you know how you'll deal with such a proposition?
- Do you really know how sexual diseases are transmitted? Do you know how best to avoid contracting such diseases?
- Have your parents or has your pastor given you an enlight-ened biblical understanding of the gift of human sexuality?
- Has anyone ever explained to you how it's possible for

love and sex to be both essential yet mutually exclusive? Do you think you understand this apparent contradiction?

- Will you panic if you're still a virgin when you graduate from college?
- Can you have friends of the opposite sex without becoming sexually involved with them?
- Will you panic if you're not engaged by the time you graduate from college? Worse yet, will you get engaged for fear that a college romance may be your "last chance"?
- Can you talk to your parents about your romantic urges and the confusion you sometimes feel?

We hope so. But we also know from sad experience that many teenagers feel abandoned when it comes to having an adult in whom they can confide their concerns about dating and getting romantically involved.

7. Suppose you've been used to being captain of the team and star of the play and soloist in the choir and at the top of the class in most of your courses. Then suppose you get to college and find out that you're surrounded by talent and you're no longer a standout.

- Are you prepared to be just a junior-varsity cheerleader or play dormitory touch football instead of making the varsity team?
- Are you prepared to be an usher instead of the leading man in the big theatrical production?
- Can you enjoy listening to somebody else's magnificently trained voice?
- Can you accept the fact that you're going to meet people vastly more brilliant, more gifted, than you? Will their giftedness inspire you to exceed your previous accomplishments, or will you sulk and claim that your talents have been overlooked?

- Will you be brave enough to experiment with your gifts and try activities you may have neglected in high school?
- Are you a self-starter, someone who can read a bulletin-board notice and decide to attend a lecture or a concert or a play or a club meeting regardless of whether or not any of your friends will go with you? Or are you wholly dependent on following somebody else's lead?

It's probable that, no matter what the quality level of your high school and no matter how often you earned praise there, you're going to meet a higher level of quality in college and as a consequence find it more difficult to gain recognition. Whether or not you benefit from these new standards of excellence is really up to you. They can lead you to soar beyond your highest expectations, or they can discourage you completely. All we can do is urge you to do your best and to be prepared to discover that your best still leaves room for improvement.

8. What if you make the team and get cast in the freshman play and pledge the sorority or fraternity of your choice and place into advanced courses and get elected to your class council and find romance in the cafeteria line . . . ?

- What if all these wonderful things happen in your first semester of college? Will you know how to choose among them, realizing that you can't do them all and do them equally well?
- Have you learned how to ask for advice and evaluate its wisdom? Or are you accustomed to going it alone, even when you know you may be in danger of making a mistake?
- Would you rather do many things fairly well or a few things extremely well?

We know many a student who spends the first two years of college trying to do it all—taking a full academic load of five courses each semester, competing on a varsity team, writing for the college daily newspaper, contributing to the yearbook, singing in the choir, and usually working at some part-time job to help with expenses. Often the predictable result is a sophomore collapse into sickness or burnout. Do you know how to avoid this unhappy consequence of trying to do it all?

College is a time for learning to make choices, for learning to be selective in the way you use your time, in the amount of energy you give to any of several conflicting obligations, in the friendships you make and the casual relationships you permit. College is a time for learning all sorts of things beyond the classroom and the labs.

The purpose of all these questions is to help you discover some things about yourself. It's not an exhaustive checklist of questions; there are certain specific areas we haven't touched on. Yet it may help you explore some of the very areas we've omitted. It may also help you and your parents open up some of the "hidden" topics—some of those subjects you haven't felt comfortable discussing.

How about it? After asking yourself these questions, would you say that you're

- ready and eager to go to college?
- open to college's challenges and opportunities?
- a little more cautious about college life than you were before?
- worried but hopeful about adjusting to college life?
- convinced it's not for you right now?

Whatever your immediate response, let's look a little more closely at what's involved in going to college.

CHAPTER 3

The Rites of Passage: Preparing for Adulthood

Ever watch a butterfly struggle to free itself from its cocoon? Or a baby chick peck its way out of its shell? Or a fledgling bird teeter on the edge of the nest? Then you know what's probably going on in your own life. But even though these years may be tough for you, they're even tougher for your parents.

WHAT'S GOING ON HERE?

What makes this period in your lives—yours and your parents'—so stressful? That's easy to answer: You and your folks are going through a wrenching experience. You're breaking loose; they're letting go. When a *juvenile* becomes an *adult*, it makes everyone a little uneasy.

It's probably been a long time since anyone dared to refer to you and your age group as "juveniles." There are fancier words to suggest the several stages you've passed through along the way, words like "pre-adolescent" and "adolescent." But the fact is that both the law and society recognize no legitimate intermediate stages. Either you're old enough to be prosecuted as an adult and get your name in the papers, or you're not; either you're old enough to get married without your parents' permission, or you're not; either you're old enough to enlist in military service, or you're not. And if you're not, you're a *juvenile.*

But not for long. Officially and by law, you'll no longer be a *minor* when you reach the age of eighteen; that's the age of *majority,* the formal way of saying you've achieved legal status as an adult. A lot is happening in your life that's leading inevitably toward the time when you're recognized as an adult and expected to carry out both the privileges and the duties of that state, such as registering to vote and casting your ballot as a fully recognized citizen.

FREEDOM AND EMANCIPATION

That's also the time when, by law, you're *emancipated* from your parents' control. Remember the Emancipation Proclamation of 1863, when President Lincoln abolished slavery in the United States? Isn't that just what you're waiting for? Maybe you're thinking that when you turn eighteen you can sleep as late as you want to without anyone—not your mom or your dad—being able to order you to the breakfast table. That when you're eighteen, you can play your stereo as loud as you want, you can go anywhere you want and stay out as late as you want . . .

But that's not really what emancipation means. There's a counterbalance to any privilege: responsibility. Emancipation doesn't mean total freedom; that would be anarchy and chaos. Emancipation means cutting loose the legal restrictions so that, instead, the law of love can bind human beings together.

When a child turns eighteen, parents are no longer *legally* responsible for housing, feeding, clothing, or educating him or her. They are responsible for supporting children under eighteen, and if they don't, they can be prosecuted for negligence. But it's not child neglect if a father decides that it's best for his son to get a job and buy his own food, or a mother decides that a daughter should buy her own clothes. This doesn't mean that emancipation automatically kicks you out the door of your parents' house, that it necessarily deprives you of their home or support. Because your folks love you, they'll probably be happy to keep you on as a member of the family for several more years. But legal statute no longer *obligates* them to you, nor you to them. The only thing that binds you is your love and respect for each other.

Similarly, after you turn eighteen, you're not obligated to disclose the contents of mail you may receive or how much you've got in your savings account. But, because you love your parents, you'll probably share this information and more; you'll probably be grateful for a roof over your head, food on the table, and clothes on your back.

In short, the law says that you and your parents can be free of obligations to each other if that's the way you want it. The point is, that's *not* the way most parents want it. And that's not really the way most teenagers want it, either. Most of us still treasure our family relationships and would like to think that they'll go on forever. But the legal possibility for separation is there, and that very possibility scares most parents to death.

This legal reality can also make some parents angry. When a school counselor tells the parents of an eighteen-year-old that he can't show them their daughter's file *unless she gives her permission,* fireworks sometimes follow. But that's the law, and the school counselor has to obey it. As for the parents, they have to learn to live with it.

JUST LIKE ANY NORMAL FAMILY

You know what happens. Your parents hover. They crowd you, suffocate you. They ask questions. They pry. They can't seem to mind their own business.

And you? You clam up. You stop talking in discernible sentences and resort to grunts and looks of disdain. Maybe you were never that talkative anyway, but now you can barely stand to be civil to any other member of the family. Or you go to your room and shut your door. You start locking your desk or your closet. You try to disappear—literally by leaving the house without a word about where you're going or when you'll be back, figuratively by hiding behind your music or your love life or your glassy-eyed staring at the TV set. You don't mean to be rude; you just need to assert the fact that you're becoming independent.

If it's any comfort to you (and your folks), this behavior is perfectly normal throughout Western civilization. Not terribly pleasant to endure, but normal. Every family goes through the same theme and variations. In fact, you might say that such behavior is part of our "rites of passage" into adulthood. The odd thing is that almost no parents can seem to remember that, when they were about fifteen or sixteen, they started acting exactly the same way that their kids are acting today.

Every culture—whether it's the Pygmies in Central Africa or the Masai in Kenya, the Tamils in South India or the Tipperahs on the Indo-Burmese border—has its own time-honored customs to prepare juvenile members of the tribe for adulthood. In some primitive tribes, boys learn how to become hunters and must spend time alone in the jungle to prove that they're not afraid of the beast, while girls learn the domestic duties of a wife and mother. In certain respects, the Jewish religious observance of bar mitzvah, by which a boy is welcomed into the privileges of Jewish manhood in the synagogue, continues the formal "rites of passage" from an ancient culture to its modern counterpart.

But for the most part, our society lacks any regulated and systematic process for passing from childhood into recognized adult standing. We have a few steps that most—but not all—young people follow, and not all in the same order or progression. And some teenagers mature faster in some ways than in others. For instance, a seventeen-year-old weightlifter may be socially immature—he hasn't had much experience with girls—but he may be extraordinarily mature in athletics; he may even be an international competitor, which is one reason why he hasn't had much time to date. So making it to adult standing— which means getting the respect of other adults and the recognition that you're one of them—may come sooner for some teenagers than for others, sooner in one area of life than in others.

TAKING STEPS TOWARD MATURITY

Responsible maturity really has more to do with *attitude* than with the number of candles on the birthday cake. If you start thinking of yourself as a responsible person, no matter how young you may be in years, you'll find that your attitude is far more mature than that of most people around you.

SHOW MATURITY BY CARING

What's the evidence of responsible maturity? Simple: it's *caring*. A responsible person cares; a careless person isn't responsible, and therefore isn't mature. The root meaning of the word "responsible" helps make the point. It comes from the Latin *sponsus*, the word for bridegroom, and *sponsa*, the word for bride. When a Roman couple came together in marriage, they vowed to care for each other, to be *re-spons*ive to each other, *re-spons*ible for each other. That's a great picture of what we mean by "responsibility."

The man who throws his trash by the side of the road isn't acting responsibly or maturely; he doesn't care about the environment in general or that neighborhood in particular. The woman who lets her poodle relieve itself on the sidewalk isn't being responsible for the same reasons. The guy who races his convertible around the bend of a rain-slicked road at 65 miles per hour isn't being responsible or mature; he doesn't care who's coming the other way or whose life he may endanger. The girl who lets her best friend hint at suicide without telling anyone about the danger isn't being either responsible or mature; she's got her loyalties confused. She cares more about keeping her friend's terrible secret than she does about saving her friend's life.

Responsible, mature adults care. What do you care about?

- your reputation for honesty?
- getting into a prestigious college?
- your freedom as a citizen of this country?
- being popular with the right crowd in school?
- your devotion to loving God?
- your success in your favorite sport?
- your family honor?
- getting the highest score on the SAT or final exam?
- downing more booze than anyone else without getting sick?
- your reliability in getting a job done well and on time?
- your loyalty to family and friends?
- driving the loudest or fastest car?
- your ability to help others in need?
- your integrity in doing your schoolwork well?
- your fair-minded attitude toward strangers?
- wearing the latest clothes?
- your duty to be a good neighbor in your community?
- having fun whenever you feel like it?
- your faithfulness in service through your church?
- scoring the winning points in the big game?
- having your own way at whatever cost to others?
- your compassion for your pet and other living creatures?
- your achievement in music, drama, or another art form?

Whatever you care about determines how responsible, how mature, your attitude will be.

SHOW MATURITY BY COMMUNICATING

Communicating is something we begin doing the moment we're born, a skill we keep refining as we mature. Communication means the exchange of information, the sharing of ideas.

Communication is the agreement arrived at between two or more people that, by language or gesture, they mean the same thing; they understand each other.

Our main means of communicating is verbal—by voice and language—although we also communicate nonverbally by gesture and facial expression. Each natural species has its sounds, but words are unique to human beings. To those who call themselves Christians, words have very special significance because Christians worship a God who speaks, who has revealed himself to the world in Christ, the Word made flesh.

Communication is one of the signs that we're human. Developing powers of communication is one of the signs that a child is growing. While a baby in a stroller is cute, we don't wish the baby—no matter how cute—to remain in that stage of life. We lament for any child who fails to grow and at three years is still like an infant, a victim of arrested development, stunted growth. Similarly, we lament for any child who never learns to speak, and we provide other means to overcome that physical or psychological handicap. Why? Because we consider talking, communicating with others to be essential to normal living.

Some young teenagers develop a communication problem. They regress and give up the power of communication. It's not that they lose the power of speech; they just decide to cut themselves off from the rest of adult civilization. Everything's in caveman grunts and sign language—or so it seems to their long-suffering parents.

This scene between a mother and her fourteen-year-old son might sound familiar to you.

"What would you like for supper?"

No reply, except for mumbling accompanied by a shrug.

"Excuse me?"

More mumbling, followed by silence.

There's a reason for this regression: some teenagers think that if they don't talk to their parents, their parents won't know what they're thinking about. And thoughts are what matter—and what reveal.

"Why won't you tell me what's on your mind?" your

mother pleads. Because it's in the treasured privacy of your imagination that you live out the fantasies and fears that are more real to you now than anything going on at home, at school, at church, on television, or in the shopping mall.

Maybe you hesitate to talk to your parents because you can't trust what their reaction might be when you tell them what's really on your mind:

- lingering worries that you're not really their child
- sexual daydreams you think may be kinky or perverted
- serious doubts about religious matters they take for granted
- occasional concerns about their marriage and its stability
- jealousy of other members of your family
- an increasingly poor self-image
- utter contempt for yourself or someone else in the family
- delusions about your own athletic or artistic skills
- questions about your reason to live

Maybe it's never occurred to you that anyone else you know—let alone your parents—might be having some of these same kinds of thoughts. The fact is that every reasonable person, including your mother and your father, has an inner conversation going on most of the time (even if they'd never admit it to you). We all live in the realm of imagination, wondering what it would be like if . . . speculating about what would happen if . . . talking to ourselves about our deepest longings and desires . . .

Little children, unsophisticated in their dealings with the rest of the world, carry on these conversations out loud. You'll hear a four-year-old talking to "her friend," sometimes inventing a different voice to identify the invisible playmate. As the child grows older and more self-conscious, those conversations stop being public. But they continue just the same, only now the voices are interior and wholly private.

This inner conversation remains hidden inside us until we find someone with whom we can be entirely intimate and honest: a friend, a lover, eventually a wife or a husband. True intimacy means finding someone with whom you can share your innermost thoughts—the hopes and aspirations you'd hardly dare to reveal to anyone you discover you're able to tell to *her*, to *him*. In such intimacy lies real communication.

How about your parents? Maybe you and your folks have just this kind of ideal relationship: you can tell them anything. But maybe you're not so sure. Could you be totally frank and honest with your father and mother? Could you talk to them about your thoughts about college? Could you tell them why you

- want to delay going to college?
- don't want to apply to the college they prefer?
- don't want to go to college at all?
- are afraid you might not succeed in college?
- don't want to prepare for the career they expect you to enter?
- don't want to attend a Christian college?
- do want to attend a Christian college?

Or are you resigned to keeping everything to yourself? Keep in mind that if you do, you're depriving yourself and your parents of the joy of sharing your thoughts, dreams, worries, and plans with them.

For the sake of this terribly important step you're about to take—going to college—we'd encourage you to try communicating with your parents. After all, it seems only fair, since any decision you make will probably affect them economically as well as emotionally.

Here are a few suggestions for improving communication between you and your parents:

1. Realize that neither you nor your parents have all the right answers.

Omniscience is the divine attribute of knowing all there is to know about everything. Human beings aren't omniscient—a fact that we should all remember and that should keep us humble.

2. Remember that it's healthy to daydream out loud.

Some of us act as if every spoken word ought to be filled with common sense or wisdom. Often we're too hard on people when we hear them talk about dreams rather than reality. What we need to keep in mind is that it's healthy to verbalize fantasies. Often it's these very fantasies that will be the springboard for a concrete plan, a solid footing from which to launch a life.

3. Don't judge your parents in advance.

You don't want your folks to assume that they know how you'll react to every situation. Why assume the same thing about them? Why hesitate to express yourself—to share your ideas or feelings—just because you're convinced your parents won't agree with you? Maybe they'll surprise you. Parents can change their minds too, you know.

4. Talk, don't argue.

If every discussion you and your parents try to have turns into a debate, ask yourself why. Maybe it's because either you or your parents seem to want conquest more than communication. How about settling for an exchange of information? How about lowering the volume and agreeing in advance that what you're going to talk about is just information for the record— a few facts and observations—not a life-changing decision? It's amazing how the tension eases when we stop arguing and start talking.

5. Remember that nature abhors a vacuum.

Most parents do too. Given a choice, most parents would rather listen to you say things they don't agree with than face a wall of silence. Even awkward communication is often better than no communication at all.

SHOW MATURITY BY CHOOSING

Caring is important and communicating is important, but making your choice clear and acting on that choice is essential. The power to *choose,* to make decisions and stick by them, is the highest level of maturity.

The rites of passage from pre-school toddler to college freshman reach their peak in the choice of that college. Following are some suggestions for how to go about making that choice.

1. Settle the issue.

As we've discussed in Chapter One, you've got to settle on the if, why, and when of going to college. Once that's done, you can move on to the next phase.

2. Start the process of elimination.

There are nearly 3,000 four-year colleges and universities in North America. You've got to talk with your parents in realistic terms about the whole business of selecting colleges and applying for admission.

What will be your basis for selecting some of them and writing to request admissions information? Will your parents decide which ones you'll write to? Will you and your parents decide that together? Will you consult your school counselor? Or will you make that decision all by yourself?

Are you planning to shoot for the top and apply to the most selective and academically rigorous colleges—Harvard, Yale, Princeton, Dartmouth, Brown, Columbia, Cornell, and Pennsylvania, the eight colleges that make up the Ivy League? How about their counterparts (once open only to women)—Radcliffe, Vassar, Smith, Mount Holyoke, Barnard, and Wellesley? What about the smaller New England colleges—Amherst, Williams, Colby, Bates, Bowdoin? Or the reputable Midwestern colleges— Carleton, Macalester, Grinnell, Coe, Oberlin, Wabash? Are you considering one of the fine Southern universities—Washington and Lee, Davidson, Duke, Baylor, Vanderbilt? What about the selective West Coast colleges—Stanford, Reed, Pomona?

What about one of the major state universities like Michigan, Virginia, North Carolina, Penn State, UCLA, California at Berkeley, or Texas. (Note: It's often very difficult for out-of-state applicants to gain admission as freshmen.)

Or do you have some more specific interests?

Are you looking for the kind of scientific specialization you'll find at Cal Tech or MIT, Rice or Drexel or Rensselaer Polytechnic Institute?

Are you interested in one of the military academies—West Point or Annapolis, the academies of the air force, coast guard, or merchant marines?

Are you looking for the advantages of an all-women's college such as Agnes Scott in Georgia or Texas Women's College or Salem College in North Carolina?

Are you hoping to enter one of the great conservatories of music such as the Juilliard School in New York City or Curtis Institute in Philadelphia or the American Conservatory in Chicago?

Would you prefer to attend a traditionally black college such as Howard University in Washington, D.C. or Fisk in Nashville or Spelman in Atlanta?

Are you considering one of the great Roman Catholic institutions such as Georgetown University, College of the Holy Cross, or College of Steubenville?

What about the evangelical Christian colleges—Wheaton, Gordon, Calvin, Houghton, Messiah, Eastern, Westmont? What about your own church's denominational college— Grove City College in Pennsylvania (Presbyterian), Evangel College in Missouri (Assemblies of God), St. Olaf's College in Minnesota (Lutheran)?

Or, if your grades and test scores aren't in a high enough range to gain you admission at a selective college, are you hoping to attend a school with a less rigorous selection policy—one of the branches of your home state's or some out-of-state university system, maybe Central Michigan or Arizona State or Southwestern Louisiana?

Are you going to apply to several different types of colleges or just the one you most want to get into? Are you tempted to apply beyond your reasonable expectations just so you can tell people, "I've applied to Harvard"?

Do you realize that it can cost up to fifty dollars just to have your application processed? These fees aren't refundable, and even if you're accepted, few colleges apply this payment toward your other costs.

3. Start thinking about finances.

Now's the time to talk to your parents about money. How much is your college education going to cost, and how is it going to be paid for?

Maybe this is the place to talk about what's really involved in college costs. Never mind what *U.S. News and World Report* or some other magazine tells you about "best bets on tuition"—you need the facts on the whole package. Here are some current price ranges:

- *tuition* (the price you pay for being allowed to attend classes and labs): at a public college if you're an in-state resident, $500-$5,000 per year; at a public college if you're an out-of-state student, $5,000-$9,000 per year; at a private college such as Williams College, $11,000 per year; at a private Christian college such as Calvin College, around $7,000 per year; at a private university such as Boston University, $12,000 per year.
- *room and board* (the cost of your dorm room and meals in the college cafeteria): $3,000-$5,000 per year.
- *fees* (anything the college wishes to add on, such as costs to cover breakage in chemistry lab, foreign-language listening tapes, computer usage, and so on): $200-$400 per year.
- *books* can run you $15-50 each, and many courses require

more than a single book. Books for a semester of five courses will cost well over $100, probably closer to $200, unless you make a point of shopping at the off-campus book exchanges that buy and sell secondhand books. But don't try to save where you shouldn't. Not buying a textbook for the sake of saving a few dollars may also mean depriving yourself of essential information, the base of a professor's instruction.

These are the bare essentials. But there are other living costs to be factored in:

- *transportation to and from college:* This expense will depend on where your college is located and how often you intend to go home. Let's guess at $200 for a nearby campus (frequent car trips) to $1000 for a distant campus (only two round-trips—fall/Christmas and New Year's/end of spring term—with no in-between trips for Thanksgiving or spring break).
- *transportation at college:* Will you need a car, or can you walk from your dorm to class? Remember, a car costs more than the price of a fill-up. You have insurance, tune-ups, repairs; and parking on campus is always a problem.
- *clothes:* Can you wear what you own, or do you need new clothes? If so, count on spending $250-500.
- *laundry/dry cleaning:* This expense will depend on how often you wash/dry clean what you wear and the prices of the facilities available to you. It might cost $10 per month; it might cost $10 per week.
- *haircuts and styling:* Hairstylists in most college towns tend to be more expensive than those back home. You can count on $15-$25 per visit.
- *food/entertainment:* This expense will depend on how much you supplement your cafeteria diet (or, if you live off-campus, how much you spend on groceries), how often you go to the movies, etc.
- *typing/photocopying services:* Most college professors don't

accept handwritten papers, and for your own peace of mind you'll probably want to make a copy of most of the papers you write. Do you type? If not, you'll pay $2-$3 per page, plus photocopying charges (ten to twenty cents a page).

- *phone bill:* This expense will depend on how often (and when) you talk to your parents and friends back home and whether your boyfriend/girlfriend is a long-distance call away.

Adding up all the items that we can estimate (and leaving transportation expenses, phone bills, etc., for you to estimate and factor in), here's the average cost of attending college in the 1990s:

Type of College or University	Average Cost per Year
public university as an in-state resident	$ 5,000
public university as an out-of-state student	9,000
private college	$16,000
private Christian college or university	$11,000
private university	$16,000

Suppose the college you most want to attend is very expensive. How do you plan to cover the costs?

—Your parents have ample financial resources to pay for your college education.

—Your parents will need to borrow some money toward your college expenses. (Most local banks or savings-and-loan associations offer college loans at low interest and ten-year repayment plans.)

—Your parents expect you to apply for financial aid from whichever college accepts you, realizing that the college may offer such aid in any of several forms:

- an outright grant based on how badly the college wants you to enroll because of your scholastic, athletic, or artistic ability

- an outright loan to be repaid to the college
- a combined grant and loan
- a guaranteed part-time job
- a combination of grant, loan, and work

—Your parents will contribute as they are able, but they expect you to work your way through college and pay most of the incidental bills yourself. Every college depends on just such students to work part-time—stocking shelves in the college bookstore, working behind the counter on the food-service line, doing desk duty in the library, filing and clerking in an administrative office, assisting in the athletic department's laundry room. Every college town hires students to mow lawns and wait on tables and deliver pizzas and provide cleaning services for offices and stores. Then there's always baby-sitting. With a little ingenuity, you can find employment to help pay those astronomical bills and keep yourself from asking for handouts at home.

4. Consider other factors.

Depending on what your financial picture looks like, you can begin to widen or narrow your choices by considering other factors:

- *Christian, church-related, secular:* What are the distinct differences among these three types of colleges? Do such distinctions matter to you?
- *co-ed or single sex:* What are the advantages and disadvantages of each? Which setting would make you more comfortable?
- *reputation in a particular department:* Are you sure enough right now about your future occupation to choose your college on that basis? Are you headed for engineering? Grove City College is strong. Medicine? Houghton College has a fine pre-med program. Hotel administration? Think

of Cornell. But what if you change your mind? Will your college be able to prepare you for a different career? Or will you have to transfer?

- *geography and climate:* How far away from home do you want to go? To what region of the country? How important are weather and climate to you? Are you an avid skier? Think about Appalachian State in Boone, North Carolina. Do you hate winter? Don't think about Appalachian State!

Choosing begins with

- talking with your parents;
- making an appointment with your school counselor;
- writing for catalogs and admissions forms (many colleges also make videotapes available to community libraries);
- planning a trip, if at all possible, to visit one or two of the campuses you expect to consider;
- attending any local college fair (colleges send their admissions representatives and recruiters to set up an exhibit booth and talk with potential applicants) and events presented by touring college groups (a choir or drama group) to see what sort of people attend that college;
- finding out when college representatives are going to visit your school, and signing up with your school counselor to meet with the ones from the colleges that interest you;
- having personal interviews (if possible) with those representatives;
- completing and mailing the application forms in the early fall of your senior year (we'll have more to say about this in the next chapter).

Caring, communicating, choosing: Those are the traits of someone who's gone through the rites of passage and moved from carefree immaturity and childish irresponsibility to the threshold of responsible adulthood.

But there are still a few more hurdles to clear.

CHAPTER 4

Clearing the Hurdles: Preparing for Admission

Edwin Moses may be the most phenomenal athlete who ever lived. After winning the 1976 Olympic gold medal in the 400-meter hurdles, Moses went for a decade without losing a race—a total of 122 races without a defeat. Included among those remarkable victories were the 1983 and 1987 World's Championships and his second Olympic gold medal in 1984. He did it every time—facing the best competition he could find—by running once around a track, in the process jumping over ten 36-inch hurdles faster and with more grace than anyone else.

Getting admitted to college is something like running a hurdles race. There's a set course to be followed and several barriers to be crossed before you finally reach your goal. You'll probably have trained professionals—like a hurdler's coach—to help you prepare for each phase of the race to college: school counselors and college-placement advisers. We'd like to think that this book will also help you along. You'll have some supporters with their own opinions to offer: your parents and relatives, along with older friends already in college, and school friends who are going through the same process with you. Learn what you can from them all. Consult with your parents; listen to their advice. But remember: It's your life, your education, and your decision—nobody else's.

GET STARTED

Start now. College admissions begin early. The best college-preparatory schools, which rely on their record of college admissions, begin to gear up in the fall of their students' sophomore year, with every sophomore taking the Preliminary Scholastic Aptitude Test (PSAT).

Did you (or will you) take the PSAT? If you don't, you not only miss a chance to warm up for a later major admissions test, but you also miss qualifying for the National Merit Scholarship (the first hurdle for that is your PSAT score). This is just one example of the importance of starting early.

Ideally, you're reading this book during the summer between your sophomore and junior years. At that point you and your parents are well-positioned to begin the long and demanding process of gaining admission to one of the colleges of your choice, the college best suited to your academic needs.

But you might be much farther along than that. Maybe you're already in your senior year—maybe this book is a Christmas present, and you've got only six more months to go before graduation—and you haven't done much of anything about college. Still, there's no need to panic. There's always a way to make up for lost time.

We've written this chapter in chronological sequence, outlining what we think is the best way to prepare for college admission. However far along you are in high school, we hope that you and your parents will be able to work your way into this sequence and start to make things happen that will result in your successful admission to college.

GET GOOD ADVICE

If you haven't already talked to your school counselor about yourself and your college ambitions, stop in at your school's counseling office and introduce yourself. Find out how your school's college-placement adviser operates. Some counselors will have a thoroughly developed program and an announced schedule for you and your parents to follow. Others may be less well-organized and, in fact, less well-informed. After reading this chapter, you'll be able to judge for yourself how much you can expect from your school's college counseling services.

Keep in mind that many high-school counseling departments are understaffed; there just aren't enough professional counselors to handle a large junior and senior class simultaneously. So, by default, such counseling departments have to limit their services just to managing the needs of the senior class. In most public high schools, those needs go well beyond college admissions. There are also students more interested in career training or technical education or military service who need assistance.

Also remember that high-school counseling involves dealing with issues far more dramatic than whether or not you get into the college of your choice. Students with eating disorders, young women facing unwanted pregnancies (some of them looking for adoption information), still other students with major problems at home, others struggling to get free from alcohol or drug addiction, some with communicable diseases, some even threatening to commit suicide—all of them looking for help from a school counselor. Is it any wonder that you may sense your school counselor is having trouble concentrating while he's talking with you about college applications? He may have just gotten off the phone with a local detox unit, where a classmate of yours is drying out.

ACT ON THE MOST IMPORTANT ADVICE

Good advice about college admission starts with good advice about your high-school program of studies. Are you enrolled in the courses intended for college applicants? Are you taking at least the minimum number of academic courses your state or your school requires a college-bound student to complete? Will you graduate with sufficient credits in

- English
- history or social studies
- mathematics
- science
- foreign language
- health and physical education

or have you been skipping some of these tougher subjects? If your academic record is uneven, let your counselor know, and find out how to improve it.

Does your school offer courses in the College Board's Advanced Placement Program? These challenging academic courses—in English, American and European history, calculus, biology, physics, chemistry, several foreign languages, art history, and studio art—reach a peak in mid-May, when three-hour exams are given in each course. (Some schools allow a student to take an APP exam on a certain subject in lieu of a final exam on the same subject.) Based on the results of those exams, a student may receive college credit or placement beyond the freshman level or both.

Sharon went from high school to the University of Virginia with enough AP course credits to be classified as a sophomore. Larry enrolled at the University of Colorado and wound up in sophomore English because of his excellent results in his high-school AP course. Not every university is so generous, but taking the AP courses in your school and doing well on the exams can be a great way to bypass basic freshman require-ments, not to mention reducing college bills.

Keep in mind that the AP exams are expensive. Most schools and school districts don't provide free testing for these optional and specialized tests. Make sure you know the current cost of registering for and taking all the AP tests you may wish to consider.

Another thing: If your school doesn't offer the Advanced Placement Program, you may want to ask your parents to look for another school for you. A good school is one that works to offer its students the best academic opportunities available.

If you want to get into a highly specialized college—for instance, if you hope to go to a scientific institute such as MIT, Cal Tech, Rensselaer, Stevens, Embry-Riddle, Webb, LeTour-neau, or one of the other high-tech campuses—you may need to insist on being placed in calculus and physics courses; you may even need to take technical drawing courses offered at a local community college or trade school. If a conservatory of music is your goal—someplace like Juilliard, Peabody, Curtis, American in Chicago, or Wheaton—you'll certainly want to make time for private instruction and participation in a per-forming group.

But even if your present expectations are narrow and fixed on a single objective for the future, by far the best advice your college-placement counselor can give you will be to get a broad-based, well-rounded high-school education. Each se-mester or term should include instruction in the liberal arts and sciences to improve your ability in reading and writing, listen-ing and speaking, reasoning and evaluating content. Well on down the road, you can begin to concentrate on computer programming or synthesizer composition or whatever other precise field of study intrigues you. But now, to lay a foundation for those studies, you need to learn what goes into making a human being unique: the arts of imagination and communica-tion; the sciences that observe, discover, measure, and record.

Your high-school counselor knows this and will help you

plan your academic program accordingly. Given sufficient time, your counselor can also help you choose the kind of electives that will give you a break from the heavy dose of high-powered academic courses your transcript needs.

READ THE BULLETIN BOARD

You can tell quite a lot about a school's college placement program by watching the bulletin board outside the counseling office. A progressive, well-informed college placement office will display

- information about admissions testing, including sign-up deadlines, costs, and testing date, time, and place;
- a variety of posters advertising colleges and universities across the country, not just those close to home;
- announcements of visits to your school by college representatives giving the date, time, and place of the meetings;
- announcements of scholarship opportunities and other financial grants you need to know about;
- announcements of college fairs scheduled nearby;
- a sign-up sheet for personal appointments with your school counselor;
- periodic reminders of approaching deadline dates.

CALENDAR OF ADMISSIONS EVENTS

Ideally, as we've said, you're reading this during the summer between your sophomore and junior years. Based on that time frame, here's the schedule we suggest.

The Fall of Your Junior Year

*1. PLAN TO ATTEND SEVERAL MEETINGS
WITH COLLEGE REPRESENTATIVES WHO COME
TO YOUR SCHOOL.*

The bulletin board outside the counseling office will tell you when and where. Even if you're not specifically interested in those colleges, hearing a few different presentations will open your eyes to what each college rep is selling.

Remember, you're a consumer, a potential buyer of educational services. Each college has something to *sell* its next group of applicants. More and more college presentations include a professionally produced videotape; all of them offer handsome brochures showing smiling faces. Be on the alert for slick but shallow presentations. Once in a long while a younger college rep misreads his audience and thinks the way to generate interest is to play down the education and play up the campus parties. That's insulting to you, a waste of your time, and you might want to tell him that. Your counselor will certainly want to know if this happens; he probably won't invite that college back anytime soon.

*2. SEND AWAY FOR INFORMATION FROM ANY
COLLEGE THAT INTERESTS YOU.*

Catalogs, brochures, viewbooks (lots of pictures, few words), sometimes even videotapes are all free for the asking. Those posters outside your school's counseling office all have postage-paid cards that you can fill in with your name and address and send without so much as licking a stamp. This may mean that your name will be put on a list of "prospects," and you may even receive a recruiting phone call as a result. But there's nothing wrong with that. At least they'll know your name.

3. START A FILE.

Get a sturdy box to hold the mass of mail that you're going to get in response to your first expression of interest in the college market. Even if you don't write to any college for a catalog, if you take a national admissions test, the SAT or the ACT, that will put you in touch with colleges that use the information from those tests for recruiting purposes. You'll get mailings from technical schools, colleges with special programs, and universities you've never seen in any ranking by the National Collegiate Athletic Association.

Use this information for comparative purposes. You might be surprised at how well some college you've never heard of stacks up against the in-state university you're considering.

The Spring of Your Junior Year

1. CHECK IN WITH YOUR SCHOOL'S COLLEGE PLACEMENT COUNSELOR.

Ask for an appointment to learn your school's procedures for helping students like you get admitted to college. Will there be individual counseling, or is everything handled in mass meetings? Is there a specific calendar your school follows? Are college-bound students automatically assigned to admissions tests, or do you have to indicate your interest in advance of each testing date? If so, do you have that schedule of dates and deadlines for test registration and payment?

After this interview, you and your counselor should have a starter list of colleges, depending on

- your current grade point average, class ranking, and any results of preliminary admissions testing;
- your indication of preferences—for a local or distant college,

for geographic region, for a public or private school, for a same-sex or co-ed school, for possible academic interests;
- your family's financial circumstances and ability to pay for college.

This initial list may surprise or perhaps disappoint you a little. Your counselor may have a current favorite college you've never heard of—someplace where he or she has earned approval from the admissions office. Or your counselor may have a few safe bets, colleges that have been hospitable to your school's graduates in the past. Don't dismiss this information. Take it and weigh it along with everything else you're learning.

And other disconcerting things might happen. Your counselor may think your grade point average isn't high enough to get you into your first-choice college; your counselor may never have heard of your aunt's alma mater and so doubt its validity as your first choice; your counselor may have been snubbed by the admissions office at your first choice and have a bias against helping anyone else try to enroll there.

Remember, college counselors are in a kind of competition all their own. They like to add up the annual score of first-choice acceptances versus first-choice rejections; they like to rate their school's acceptance/rejection ratio at the highly selective colleges. So they're reluctant to have students apply to colleges they think the students won't have a good chance of getting into; it hurts their statistics. But you're the one going to college, not the the counselor. Of course you want to be realistic about your choices, but it's up to you to become informed, know your options, and make your decisions accordingly.

2. CONSULT SOME COLLEGE-COMPARISON HANDBOOKS.

We've deliberately chosen not to compile any list or ranking of colleges and universities we know and consider strong choices. But such books are available, and their information can be highly useful if taken with a grain of salt. Remember that most college guides represent the individual preferences and prejudices of their authors and so will be helpful to you only insofar as you share those tastes.

Your school counselor will have a collection of these books in the guidance office; you can also find them in your school or community library. We've compiled a list of books in Chapter Eleven; here are just a few titles from that list:

- *Barron's In-Depth Profiles of American Colleges* (Barron's Educational Series)
- *Comparative Guide to American Colleges,* Cass and Birnbaum (Harper & Row)
- *How to Get an Ivy League Education at a State University,* Nemko (Avon)
- *Lovejoy's Concise College Guide,* Straughn and Straughn (Monarch Press)
- *Peterson's Consider a Christian College* (Peterson's Guides)
- *Selective Guide to Colleges,* Fiske (Times Books)
- *The College Handbook,* edited annually by the College Board (College Board)

In fact, the College Board puts out a whole series of very helpful publications. Your counselor will be able to show you a catalog indicating current availability.

3. ASK ABOUT COMPUTER-SOFTWARE PROGRAMS THAT CLASSIFY COLLEGES.

If you happen to have access to a computer and prefer working its keyboard to paging through books, investigate prepackaged programs that will categorize hundreds of colleges and universities according to their principal characteristics. Say you want to know about a small, co-ed, liberal arts college that's located in a rural environment but has an urban studies program. Access the information from a software program and up will pop dozens, scores, even hundreds of colleges that fit your specifications. This information doesn't describe or compare colleges; it doesn't pit one against the other. It simply groups them, uncritically, according to various traits.

Here are three software programs we're familiar with:

- *The College Board's College Explorer*
- *The College Board's College Entry*
- *Peterson's College Selection Service*

4. BE SURE YOU'VE SIGNED UP FOR THE SPRING SERIES OF TESTS OFFERED BY THE COLLEGE BOARD AND AMERICAN COLLEGE TESTING.

If your school uses the College Board tests, you'll be taking the infamous three-hour Scholastic Aptitude Test (SAT) in the spring; you should also be taking the one-hour Achievement Tests, which are offered in Mathematics I, the sciences (biology, chemistry, physics), American or European history, and English composition. Most colleges expect you to submit scores from three of the tests; colleges may or may not specify which test scores to submit. Some high schools also use these tests as a means of checking up on how well their teachers and students are doing in national rankings.

By the way, you need to know that, as of this writing, the College Board offers only once each year—usually in December—its English composition achievement test in a form different from that of its other tests. Instead of testing exclusively by multiple-choice problems in writing, the December test also asks you to write an essay on an assigned topic. Sometimes the topics are a little weird:

"The trouble with being open-minded is that your brains may fall out. Based on your reading, observation, and experience, write a 20-minute essay in which you comment on this statement."

You don't have much time—a total of twenty minutes in which to think about and write your essay. If you're better at writing than you are at solving A-B-C-D or none-of-the-above standardized test questions, you may want to be sure to take this test. Also, check to see if the colleges you're interested in may be among those requiring the results of the written essay.

The Summer Before Your Senior Year

1. TRY TO TAKE A COLLEGE TOUR.

It's time to get down to business, and if it's at all possible, you ought to pay a visit to at least two or three of those colleges to which you intend to apply. It's best to take this kind of trip before your senior year. According to our calendar, the trip would be scheduled for the summer before that year, but if you can arrange a trip over the winter or spring break of your junior year or even over Memorial Day weekend, so much the better.

Don was a nationally ranked high-school athlete and knew that numerous colleges would be recruiting him. He wanted to visit a lot of these campuses, so he arranged his tour in three different stages. Just before his junior year, he flew to Chicago and met his parents there, then drove with them from Illinois through Indiana (with a detour into Michigan and back), then on through Ohio, Pennsylvania, New Jersey, and home to New York. En route, he spent a brief time on the campuses of Wheaton, Northwestern, the University of Chicago, Notre

Dame, Michigan State, Michigan, Alma, Albion, Hillsdale, Bowling Green, Malone, Kent State, Westminster, Grove City, Bucknell, Lehigh, Lafayette, Princeton, and Rutgers—all in one Friday-to-Monday stretch!

The next fall he went south to visit Covenant College in Chattanooga, Duke, and the University of North Carolina at Chapel Hill. Finally, in the spring of his senior year, when the pressure to choose was mounting, he made return visits to Princeton and Wheaton, but he also spent time at the University of Pennsylvania and the University of Missouri.

By the time he narrowed down his choices, Don had seen about two-dozen campuses and had slept overnight, eaten, and been interviewed at a third of them. In the end he applied to eight before choosing Chapel Hill.

Not everyone can have the luxury of so much window-shopping. And not everyone needs to sample so broadly. Don's brother Kevin was just as widely recruited as an athlete, but he visited only two colleges and applied only to the one he eventually attended, joining his brother at UNC. Their younger sister Ellyn did much the same thing, visiting a few colleges (Salem, Sweet Briar, Virginia, and Mary Washington) on her way home from visiting her brothers at school, then applying to only two and being accepted by both before making her choice: UNC.

The point is that it's helpful to visit at least a few colleges before making your choice.

Not that it's going to be a disaster if you don't visit a school before enrolling there. Cindy went to Wheaton from her home in Kenya, East Africa (her parents were missionaries). She'd spent no time whatever at Wheaton before arriving there as a freshman, but she had no trouble adjusting to her new surroundings. Similarly, her sister Sandy arrived in this country from overseas and just a few days later was on the campus of Taylor University for the first time and adjusted well.

But their younger sister Diane spent six years in this country before going to college. After visiting several campuses, she enrolled at Messiah College (not her first choice, by the way) and was miserable for much of her freshman year. She seriously considered transferring but changed her mind when a certain young man entered her life. Now, several years after graduation, Diane and Dave are still at Messiah College, where he's a member of the physical education department and coaching staff, while Diane works in public recreation.

These examples simply show that everybody's different. But as a rule, most of us feel more comfortable leaving home if we know a little about our destination and what to expect when we get there. So a visit to your possible college campus is a good idea if you can afford it and arrange it.

2. TAKE A CASUAL TOUR, OR MAKE A FORMAL APPOINTMENT.

You don't need to make a big production out of your college visit. You can simply walk the campus and look over the community. Most colleges and universities are remarkably open (although we do know a couple of institutions with guards at the gates), and so it's usually quite easy to wander through the public areas such as the student union, the library, the chapel (many colleges have elegant chapels, though some are no longer used for worship as such), and classroom buildings. The residence halls are something else. Don't assume that you can look through a dormitory without first checking in at the hall director's office or apartment.

As you walk around, here are a few things to look for:

- Do students and faculty or staff appear to be friendly, at least to each other if not to you as a stranger?
- Does anybody take the time to ask if you need help in finding your way? Are you recognized as a visitor and potential candidate for admission?

- Are the buildings and grounds in decent condition? Are there signs of ongoing maintenance? Or are things generally in a state of disrepair?
- Do the classroom buildings seem conveniently located near the library, student union, chapel, and other sites of daily activity? Are the classroom buildings close together, or do you have to take a bus to get from one building to the next?
- Where are the dorms in relation to the dining hall and the classroom buildings? Is where you'd live within walking distance of where you'd eat?
- Does typical classroom seating suggest a moderate number of students in each class, or are most of the classrooms set up like large lecture halls? You can tell a lot about the style of a college's instruction by the classroom configuration.
- When you walk through the library, do you get a sense that serious business is going on there? Or is it more like an overflowing TV lounge in one of the dorms?
- How many out-of-state license plates can you spot in the parking lot? Does the number suggest that the school draws students primarily from within the state, or that the school has a mix of students from all over the country?
- Do the stores and restaurants near the campus seem to welcome the college students, or is there tension between them?
- Do you get a good feeling just being on this campus? Or is there something cold or even awkward about the spirit you feel there?

You can make your visit more formal, of course. Most colleges and many universities will grant you an interview if you plan your visit at a convenient time of the year and write or call ahead. Even though it may be your spring vacation, never expect to be welcome during the end of March or the beginning of April, when the most selective colleges are trimming their lists prior to sending out their acceptance notices. This is a time when they're just too busy to deal with anyone other than the immediate group of applicants.

Assuming you've chosen a better time of year, when you call or write, ask to meet with an admissions counselor and ask if a student guide can take you on a tour of the campus.

When you talk with the counselor, ask about the college's strengths in the particular academic department that most interests you. Ask how many freshman and sophomore courses are taught by the college's most experienced teachers, and how many are taught by graduate students or young faculty still trying to finish their own graduate studies. If you're already thinking about your post-college future, ask about the college's record of its graduates' admission to post-graduate professional schools—medical, law, engineering, business. Ask about its graduates' record of winning major recognition, such as a Rhodes Scholarship to Oxford or a Woodrow Wilson Fellowship.

Ask about the non-academic learning environment the college offers—lectures by famous speakers, concerts and recitals by a wide variety of musicians, fairs or festivals for the folk arts. Ask how many international students are enrolled.

Don't forget to ask about the food service and the several plans available, as well as your options for eating elsewhere. And ask about the housing policies. Are freshmen guaranteed on-campus accommodations? If so, how many occupants to a room? If not, what are the alternative living arrangements? A nephew named Matt is a freshman at Rutgers, the state university of New Jersey. He has a room in the freshman dorm, but over Christmas vacation he had to empty his room of all his belongings, then move them all back in in mid-January. Why? College policy, that's all. Next year he has to move out of the dorm and live with four other students in an apartment complex. If Matt had known these details in advance, he might have reconsidered enrolling at Rutgers. Now he's looking into the possibilities of transferring.

If the college is an evangelical institution, or even if it only claims to be "church-related," be sure to ask about the spiritual tone of the campus. If the college talks about its commitment to Christian education, what does it expect of its students and faculty in terms of Christian behavior? Are you comfortable with these expectations? Will you be able to keep your word and conform to the college's code of standards, even if it restricts you more than your own parents do? How much emphasis is given to communal worship? Is chapel attendance required or voluntary? How much evidence is there of service to others?

Even if the college isn't particularly religious, is there still a place for student groups that pay attention to spiritual concerns? Is there a chaplain on the faculty or in the student affairs office?

Ask about the social dimension of college life. Are students generally made to feel welcome in their professors' offices? Are students ever invited to their professors' homes? Is there an amicable relationship between male and female students, or is everyone engaged in sexual politics? Do you have to be a fraternity or sorority member to qualify for a position in student leadership? Do parties involve heavy drinking, or does the college take the legal drinking age seriously? What's the college doing to combat the influence of drugs on campus and in the community? Is the campus a safe place to walk at night, or are there security problems?

Scott enrolled at a technical college in the heart of an inner city's depressed area. As part of his freshman orientation, he and his new classmates were given instruction in personal defense—the college's indirect way of saying, "This isn't a very safe neighborhood." It's better to know about things like this in advance.

The basketball team may be nationally ranked, the campus may be listed among the loveliest in America, the Environmental Protection Agency may approve of the water supply. The admissions counselor will want to tell you about all these points of pride. But your primary concern ought to be the ways in which this particular college will suit your needs—educational, physical, spiritual, and social.

3. THINK ABOUT COLLEGES.

When you were a kid, you probably started thinking about Christmas pretty soon after Labor Day. Do the same now about college. Make where you're going to college a priority. Start thinking *now* about what characteristics you most want in a college.

4. TALK ABOUT COLLEGES.

Use your reading, visits, interviews, and your friends' experiences to compare and contrast your first choice with other colleges. Exchange opinions with your friends and listen to their observations. Make sure you know why you're leaning toward one college over all the others. If all your friends are going somewhere else, you may want to reassess your choice.

5. DREAM ABOUT COLLEGES.

Don't be afraid to use your imagination to help you decide what you most want from a college. Pretend you've been accepted at the college you most want to attend. What are you doing there? What courses are you studying? Where are you living? Who's your roommate? Are you succeeding academically? socially? spiritually?

6. PRAY ABOUT COLLEGES.

Do you believe that God holds you in his love? Then this same God cares about your college choice. Pray for guidance to make the right decisions in the choices that soon will face you.

CHAPTER 5

The Final Push: Preparing for Anything

As some of your older friends may have warned you, the days of your senior year will pass all too quickly. Looking back, you'll almost certainly agree that the weeks from Labor Day to Thanksgiving just seemed to evaporate. Then it's Christmas, and almost instantly half of your wonderful senior year—that golden time you were going to treasure—has slipped away. Before it does, make sure you've made some more progress on your college admissions work.

THINGS TO DO DURING THE FALL AND WINTER OF YOUR SENIOR YEAR

1. Recheck to make sure that your academic courses are targeted to give you a college-entrance diploma.

Remember, it's ultimately your responsibility to be sure that you're taking the right courses to reach your goal. You may discover that you're deficient in a particular requirement and have to overload your academic schedule in the fall—you may even have to enroll in a night course or community college to get that needed credit. This will be tough but not impossible. The important thing is to be properly prepared when you graduate.

2. Having narrowed your choices from all 3,000 colleges to only a handful, write to those that most interest you and request application forms.

Asking for application forms from a small group of colleges is the equivalent of making your first cut. You've eliminated about 2,995 other possible choices. Now all you have to do is pare down your choices to a single college.

Your letter doesn't need to be an essay. Something as simple as this will do:

Date

Office of Admissions
College or University
Street
City, State ZIP

To Whom It May Concern:

Please send me a complete application packet, including financial aid information and appropriate forms.

I anticipate applying for admission as a freshman, entering in September 1993.

My name and address appear below.

Yours truly,

Your name
Street
City, State   ZIP

A SPECIAL NOTE ON "EARLY DECISION"

Certain colleges offer a special feature in their admissions program called "early decision." A student participating in "early decision" applies to only one of these colleges and thereby commits himself or herself to enroll in that college if accepted. *Completed applications must be postmarked by November 1.* This plan enables a college to identify applicants who are the most eager and often the most capable. Students who participate in this plan help a college pick the cream of its crop of applicants.

But be careful—"early decision" involves making a promise that should be kept. Be sure you really want to go to that one-and-only choice because, if you're accepted, you've made a moral commitment to be there. Most colleges take these agreements very seriously. One or two of the most selective colleges can afford to be generous if you change your mind, but for the most part, if you back out of the decision you've made, you'll find some unhappy admissions officers at two colleges—the one you've rejected and the one you're now trying to get into.

3. Listen to your school counselor's advice about completing the application forms:

- how to answer specific questions;
- how to write the essay that may be required;
- how to choose personal references to support your application.

Your school counselor will have his or her own advice on each of these matters. All we'll add is this:

- Don't be cute or smart-alecky or presumptuous; don't be dramatic or corny ("I have yearned from earliest childhood

to stand among the tall and the proud who wear the Maize and Blue of Michigan").
- Don't copy an essay out of a book of canned essays— somebody's commercial attempt to solve your problem by writing your essay for you. Several books of these pre-digested essays exist, and every college admissions officer is aware of them and can recognize a canned essay at first glance.
- Don't choose a "bad risk" to write a letter of reference for you. If you don't get along very well with a particular teacher, don't ask him or her to recommend you. Try to avoid choosing a procrastinating teacher to write a letter of reference. If your teacher is regularly overdue in returning graded papers or exams, he would probably treat your letter the same way, and your application would suffer as a result.

4. If you need financial aid, research the possibilities of applying for particular scholarships.

Your school counselor will have books listing scholarships, grants, and loans from thousands of sources. These funds are available to "deserving and qualified applicants"—a phrase that means different things to different donors. One scholarship is open only to orphans living in Appalachia; another scholarship is available only to persons of Icelandic heritage; another goes to the applicant whose parents are both currently in jail; still another goes to someone with an interest in box turtles. Aid is also available to the children of veterans or former POWs, to daughters of sorority members, to children of Rotarians, to persons committed to preparing for Christian service. The list is endless and endlessly varied.

If you're a member of any officially declared minority— Native American, black, Hispanic, Asian, or female—or if you have a physical handicap, you should certainly be looking carefully for the many sources of financial assistance newly available under federal guidelines. For more information, check the bibliography in Chapter Eleven or ask your school counselor.

Many states offer financial grants exclusively to their own high-school graduates, but you need to know the qualifying terms. Is there a special test to take, or do you submit the scores from some other national test? Does the grant apply to any college in the country or only to in-state colleges? In the latter case, does it apply to any college in your state or only to a limited group of public colleges (a tricky way for the state to improve its admission ratio of more highly capable students to its own less desirable colleges)? What's the deadline for applying?

Besides looking through your counselor's books, check the bulletin board for flyers from various colleges and universities announcing their special scholarship opportunities.

A WORD TO POTENTIAL ALL-AMERICA NOMINEES

If you're a standout athlete, you'll want to read the glossary entry under "grant-in-aid." But here we want to say a few things about how to go about applying for that grant-in-aid and what happens if you get it.

The National Collegiate Athletic Association (NCAA), the largest governing body for intercollegiate athletics, oversees the fair recruiting of potential All-America athletes and the equitable distribution of financial grants to those chosen. At this writing, the NCAA has three divisions. Division I is the most competitive; its members are the universities whose teams we see most often on TV. To get into Division I competition, you have to be a state qualifier in your sport, if not an Olympic prospect.

Division II is for colleges wishing to compete at a level just below that of Division I, somewhat less intensely committed to big-time sports. Nonetheless, some excellent teams and individual athletes compete in Division II. Division III also attracts many fine athletes but offers no direct financial aid for athletic participation; several of the leading Christian colleges compete at the Division III level.

The NCAA has very strict regulations about the recruiting of athletes and the financial assistance they're offered in return for playing their sports. The NCAA's first consideration isn't how great an athlete you are but whether or not you meet certain standards as a student. For more information on the NCAA's qualifications, check the glossary in Chapter Eleven (see "NCAA Proposition 48").

There are also ethics to be upheld and explicit recruiting rules to be followed. In fact, the NCAA differentiates between *unethical, irregular,* and *illegal* recruiting devices. For instance, it's unethical of a college to pester a star athlete with late-night phone calls, especially from sultry-voiced co-eds encouraging him to meet them on their campus. But it's a violation of regulations for an influential alumnus to call and apply pressure; and it's downright illegal for any college representative to send money, plane tickets, or other valuables to an athlete or other members of his family as an inducement to get him to enroll. A college can be severely penalized—even lose the right to field a team—for breaking these rules.

The NCAA permits a Division I athlete to receive a grant-in-aid consisting of all or part of the following package:

tuition and fees
room and board
allowance for books
per diem expenses incurred while traveling to compete
a limited number of free tickets to games

How much the athlete is offered will depend on the coaching staff's estimate of his potential value to the team or on how many grants to other athletes have already been awarded and what's left to offer him.

The NCAA does not permit an athlete to use the coach's

telephone to make long-distance calls or allow an enthusiastic alumnus to express his appreciation by offering the athlete a new convertible or new clothes.

Division II athletes receive a smaller package of benefits; Division III athletes compete for the love of their sports.

Your school coach or athletic director should be able to advise you properly and protect you from any unscrupulous recruiting tactics. If you believe that you have college-level ability, start by writing directly to the coach at every college on your list—not to college admissions officers. Don't send your your whole scrapbook of clippings and awards. A college coach needs only a one-page synopsis of your performances and accomplishments. If you don't get a response from the college athletic department, call and tell the coach about your athletic achievements; ask him or her to send you application forms. If you get no response again, accept the message that your abilities don't measure up to that particular college's standard of competition, at least not well enough for you to merit a financial grant.

But that's not necessarily the end of your athletic career. If you still want to attend that college, proceed with the usual admissions program. If you get accepted and want to try out for the team, let the coach know you're coming as a freshman, ask to be put on the summer mailing list, and ask for the team's summer conditioning recommendations. That way he or she knows you're a serious athlete. Introduce yourself at the early season meeting, attend practice faithfully, and be willing to carry the water bucket if necessary. Many so-called walk-on athletes end up with both a varsity letter and a financial grant.

If you intend to compete as a college athlete, even in a low-key program that never makes it to ESPN, you need to be aware of its demands on your time and energy. Academic scheduling often conflicts with athletic practice and competition time. You'll need to juggle eating times and study hours, allowing for recuperation from strenuous workouts. You may even have to take a lighter academic load during your competitive season or go to summer school to make up missing credits. And remember that college competition usually involves traveling longer distances than your high-school "away" games may have. So you'll have to figure jet lag or long, bumpy bus rides into your schedule.

These are matters every college athlete must face. But it's also important to face the fact that, despite all the positive features of college sports, there's an ugly side to it that we see all too often. Although the NCAA guidelines are clear and readily available, every year we read about major violations by famous coaches or their unknown assistants; we read about a university losing its television coverage and income by being banned from playing in a New Year's Day bowl game. What we don't read about is the damage done to the athletes, whose main—and maybe wrongheaded—reason for enrolling at that university was only to play on its football or basketball team. We don't read about the many athletes who never receive a diploma and degree, who leave college uneducated, if not illiterate, incapable of holding a secure job.

Don't mistake us for being anti-sports. We believe in the value of college athletics. Both of us were athletes in and after college; our sons and daughters were all college athletes (two of them have been college coaches); one son-in-law coaches a nationally ranked Division III soccer team. But we want to caution you: *Don't sell your soul for the sake of a coach's promises.* Get your varsity letter if you can; win your NCAA medals and your All-America certificate if you're able to. And go on to greater victories if talent and opportunity allow it.

Above all, enjoy the game. But be sure to leave your last game or match with your integrity unblemished, your body, mind, and spirit unbroken by the stress of chasing after a gold, silver, or bronze phantom called *glory.* For every athlete, after a while, the medals and trophies have a way of tarnishing; only honor and character developed through fair play remain.

5. When you're close to completing your applications, request that your school counselor send official transcripts (academic records) to the several colleges you've selected.

Your academic records—including your class ranking, grade-point average, and test scores—are the most important credentials you have to present to the several colleges to which you're applying. But you won't be mailing your own transcript to any of these colleges. Only your school counselor is entrusted by your school with the responsibility of transmitting accurate and honest records to colleges, military officials, future employers, and anyone else who has legitimate reason to request them. Transcripts are official only when stamped with the school's seal or otherwise shown to be authentic.

Transcripts are also legal documents. They bear the weight of your school's integrity, as indicated by the official seal, affirming that the grades and class ranking recorded are the correct and official record of your academic work.

6. Once you've carefully chosen the best people to recommend you, ask teachers, coaches, administrators, your pastor, or other adults who know you well to complete a recommendation for you.

If someone agrees to help you, make it as easy for her or him as you can. Some of your teachers will be asked to complete many such recommendations. They can't possibly keep track of which student is applying to which college. You've got to lend a hand. Here's what you do:

- Don't ask at the last minute. A month's notice is a good idea.
- Don't make a busy person guess whose form he or she is

working on. Give every person you ask a copy of the college's recommendation form with all the information about you, *including your name,* already filled in.
- Provide a stamped envelope already addressed to the proper college. Your references are mailed directly by the people who write them.
- Be grateful. A little courtesy will certainly be appreciated.

7. Mail your completed applications.

If you've decided to apply under the "early decision" ground rules (see the glossary), then you know that your applications have to be postmarked by November 1. If you're willing to be part of the larger pool of candidates, you can wait another few months. But if you want to avoid last-minute pressure and give yourself a Christmas present at the same time, get all your applications in the mail by Christmas Eve.

With each application, don't forget to include the check or money order for each college's application fee. Part of your ongoing communication with your parents will be this matter of money: Who pays for what? How many application fees are you willing to pay? Remember, most colleges don't refund the application fee or count it toward your total costs, so you may want to limit your applications accordingly. It's up to you and your folks to decide.

8. Sign up for a second round of admissions aptitude testing.

All the way through your senior year, you can submit the best test scores you receive, so retaking the exam may very well be to your advantage. If you took the exam last spring and didn't like your results, maybe you should take it again. The experience of already having taken the tests and your greater maturity (not to mention your increased wisdom as a high-school senior) may help elevate your scores.

WHAT ABOUT COACHING FOR THE SAT?

This may not be the place to debate whether coaching for the SAT and other admissions tests really helps, but we wanted to offer a few brief comments.

All successful test-taking is an acquired skill. The SAT, the ACT, and other national standardized tests require that you become familiar with the various sorts of problems each test presents. You learn how to answer true/false statements, you learn how to fill in the blanks, you learn how to solve algebra or geometry problems.

If you're having trouble mastering these skills, you may be able to improve your scores on these tests by several means:

- buy one of the many workbooks available and plod your way through each example of a verbal or mathematical test;
- enroll in the special classes your school offers in preparation for admissions testing;
- concentrate your energies on doing well day-by-day in your regular schoolwork, including each test your teachers give;
- sign up with a commercial coaching firm and pay a hefty fee for ten or twelve hours of instruction in how to beat the tests;
- take the tests repeatedly on the theory that "practice makes perfect."

Which technique works best? The answer is all, some, or none of the above. There's no doubt that becoming familiar with the several methods of testing—verbal analogies, for instance—improves your confidence and thereby your score. But simply facing the same firing squad every time the tests are given or drilling the formula for a verbal analogy into your head for hours on end is no guarantee that you really understand how to reason and recognize why a window in a house is analogous to the eye in the body.

So, while a testing expert (by the way, most commercial firms don't have "experts"—they're simply classroom teachers working after-hours) may help you overcome handicaps to success, the best way to improve your test scores is to apply yourself to all your schoolwork and watch your scores rise accordingly. As you read better and comprehend more, your reading and sentence-completion components on the admissions test will improve; as you complete your math homework faithfully and master the principles of trigonometry or calculus in your regular math class, your math component on the test will improve.

Your improvement may not be so dramatic as the improvement newspaper ads claim they can help you achieve, but it will be authentic, a truer measure of what you know than the result of a quick fix from a testing tutor would be.

WINTER AND SPRING OF YOUR SENIOR YEAR: WHAT TO DO WHILE YOU WAIT FOR RESULTS

If you've chosen the "early decision" program, you'll hear from your only college choice before Christmas. Otherwise, most of the colleges you've applied to won't begin responding until mid-winter or early spring. What do you do in the meantime?

1. If you and your parents require financial aid to meet your college expenses, you need to apply for it.

The official papers are called the Financial Aid Form (see the glossary) and can be picked up in your guidance office. Soon after January 1, your parents will receive their W-2 forms from their employers, showing last year's earnings and the taxes withheld. This information, along with other information found in their tax return for the previous year, will be needed to fill out the FAF.

Many colleges will also require your parents to use a financial-aid clearinghouse agency called College Scholarship Service (see the glossary). For a small fee, this agency interprets a family's financial resources and recommends how much aid a student will need to make ends meet. Then, if the college accepts that student, it's up to the college to put together its offer of an outright grant or full scholarship, or of a combination of partial grant or scholarship, loan, and guaranteed part-time job.

2. Sometime before your school's mid-winter break, check back with your counselor to be sure that

- your transcripts have been sent to the correct list of colleges (Was it Washington and *Lee* or Washington and *Jefferson?* Was it Wheaton in *Illinois* or Wheaton in *Massachusetts?* Was it Cornell *College* in Iowa or Cornell *University* in New York?);
- your counselor hasn't received any notice from your colleges that they're missing any recommendations required for your application. (This is a way to check up on a procrastinator.)

3. Be patient.

The longest two or three months of your life are about to begin. Many colleges conduct what they call "rolling admissions," which means that they accept students throughout the year until they reach their limits. Other colleges maintain a more rigid schedule, informing everyone at once, usually after March 1. The most selective colleges and universities—the Ivy League and others of equal standing—observe a uniform date of April 15 to mail their notices of each applicant's status: accepted, rejected, or put on a waiting list.

4. Don't panic.

Just because your best friend got accepted last month and you haven't heard yet doesn't necessarily mean anything. It doesn't mean that nobody wants you, that you'll be rejected everywhere you applied. Give it time. Everybody else is just as anxious as you are.

CHAPTER 6

Getting Serious:
Preparing for Acceptance

THE LETTER'S IN THE MAIL

The whole wearying process of college admissions reaches its climax on the day(s) you receive your letters of notification from those colleges to which you've applied. If you've chosen to go the "early decision" route (explained in the previous chapter, as well as in the glossary), you won't have long to wait for the news. If you've gone the more traditional route, the news won't come so quickly. The most selective colleges and universities generally wait to send out their letters on April 15, which means a relatively long and tension-filled wait; other colleges have their own schedules. But all of them keep you in suspense far longer than you'd think bearable.

The waiting is especially stressful if there's more at stake than just whether or not a student gets accepted to a college. If his or her acceptance is a status symbol—and if rejection means *personal* rejection—then we're talking real trouble. That's the way it often is at the most competitive college-preparatory schools, public or private. The days following April 15 are filled with such anxiety that normal routines are shattered. A friend who is an administrator at one of the most hard-driving day schools in New York City tells us that his school has to allow for extraordinary tension among its seniors, leading in some instances to near nervous collapse. Students rush to the pay phones and call home at the hour they expect the mail to have been delivered. When the maid or a parent brings the letter to the phone, the anxious student first doesn't want it opened, then does.

"We sometimes bring in extra psychological counselors," our friend tells us, "just to be prepared in case we have an epidemic of rejections at Harvard. Some of our kids would be downright suicidal if their letters brought bad news."

In a society in which going to college has now become the norm for a majority of high-school graduates, some young people face added pressures imposed by their status-seeking parents. For such parents, it's not enough that their daughter or son attend college; that daughter or that son must be accepted by a prestigious college or university with a reputation for exclusive admissions and a record of placing its graduates in elite graduate schools or opening the doors to high-paying corporate positions.

We know of many such cases: young men whose fathers' dreams have projected them into starting positions on an Ivy League or Big Ten varsity team; young women whose adoring parents see their daughters only as homecoming queens at their alma maters where they met and fell in love; mediocre students whose successful mothers or fathers expect far more than is reasonable. Often these parents seem to possess little or no real understanding of their children's academic, athletic, or artistic potential; they've never been able to accept and rejoice in the fact that their children are wonderful human beings—not as talented as some, but still worthy of respect nonetheless.

When parents' aspirations for their children run too far ahead of reality, the burden can be unbearable.

"I'll never be able to satisfy my dad," a boy named Paul once told us. "He's everything I'm not: super-intelligent, a great college athlete, and successful in his business. Me? I mess up everything I touch. Why can't he just take me as I am?"

That was thirty years ago. You won't be surprised to learn that Paul has lived a miserable life, including divorce, drug addiction, a jail sentence, and alienation from his parents and his own children. Of course, for much about these sorry circumstances Paul himself is responsible. But we believe that, to some degree, his father's stubborn refusal to grant Paul the right to achieve at his own level—to let his positive qualities as well as his limitations shape his life—contributed most to Paul's personal collapse.

TIME TO MAKE A DECISION

You thought it would never happen, but one day your waiting is over.

Maybe it's a pre-Christmas day when your "early decision" announcement arrives. If you took a different application route, perhaps it's a late winter day in March or an early spring day in April. Maybe it's during your Easter vacation, and you happen to be at home when the mail arrives. Something tells you that today's the day. You feel a tingle of anticipation as you thumb through the pile of flyers, bills, and letters addressed to other members of your family.

Then you find it: an embossed envelope bearing the name of your first choice in the upper left corner, addressed to you.

But wait a minute. There's a second letter addressed to you, this one from your second choice.

Before you reach this point, you should settle a couple of issues.

1. If I'm accepted at more than one college, do I have any plan for deciding on one and turning down the others? Am I sure why I've set my heart on my first choice?

Have you drawn up a list of advantages and disadvantages for each of your colleges? Have you ranked those advantages in a way that makes your first choice rise to the top of every list? Where does your second choice fit in your priorities? What attracts you to that school? And what about the local college? Does it have special advantages you shouldn't overlook?

If you haven't already done so, take time to make a list of preferences, ranking them (1, 2, 3) according to your taste. Be tough on yourself and on the colleges you're considering. This is no mere popularity contest; it's a major decision with some major consequences. If you don't have something concrete like this list, you may simply be following some emotional tug that draws you toward one particular institution over all the others. Maybe it's intuition; maybe it's a matter of how comfortable you were made to feel during your visit to the campus; or maybe your religious experience has taught you to interpret God's will for your life through how you feel about such things. Such feelings are important, but they need to be supported by clearheaded thinking.

Your list might look something like this, give or take a few factors:

	FIRST CHOICE	SECOND CHOICE	LOCAL COLLEGE
Location	1	3	2
Cost	3	2	1
Selectivity	1	2	3
Academic Quality	1	2	3
Academic Difficulty	1	2	3
Social Life	1	2	3
Housing	1	2	Live at home
Food	1	2	Eat at home

Job Opportunities	2	3	1
Social Support (friends I know there)	1	3	2
Spiritual Support	2	3	Home church

Based on a ranking even as simple as this, can there be any doubt where your heart's desire lies? Except for cost, it's clearly no contest between your first choice and the other two. If your first choice is also the most expensive choice, you need to weigh the cost factor seriously and figure out how to pay the bill (if you haven't already).

In any case, it's a good idea not to wait until your letters arrive to line up your best reasons for preferring one college over the others.

2. If I'm not accepted at my first choice, am I ready to accept that disappointment and consider alternatives?

Tough as it seems to take, you'll more likely than not be turned down by your first choice, no matter how much of a sure thing you and your parents and your school counselor think you are. For instance, at this writing, the University of Virginia accepts fewer than one out of every four applicants; Harvard and Stanford take only 15 percent of all applicants; the U.S. Naval Academy invites only one out of every ten applicants to enroll.

So expect the best while preparing for the worst. Of course it will hurt if your first choice turns you down, but it helps to put this experience in perspective. Of all the potential kinds of pain a human being can endure, getting a polite rejection from a college has to be among the most temporary. If you're a positive and forward-looking person, you'll get over your initial hurt. It's not the end of the world, and it's not to be taken as a judgment of you personally. You're not inferior to those who were accepted. In fact, if you recall what we said at the end of Chapter One, it's altogether likely that the reason you weren't accepted has more to do with other people than it does with you. Many of those rejected are no less qualified than those who are accepted.

3. What if I'm accepted at my second choice? Can I enroll there in a happy frame of mind, or will I still be feeling rejected and carrying a chip on my shoulder?

When you ask this question, remember that this is the college that wants *you*. It was good enough when you applied, so why not accept its offer of admission with thanks and make up your mind to succeed there?

There's no real point in carrying a chip on your shoulder. Get on with your life. If you're extremely disappointed, you can always reapply to your first choice after a semester or two of good work at your second choice. Some students do just that. But many others who intend to transfer discover, after a year or two, that they've never been happier, and they decide to stay right where they are.

WHAT THE LETTERS WILL SAY

When your mail actually arrives, those letters will convey one of three messages:

- you've been accepted
- you've been put on a waiting list and have to wait for another month or more
- you've been rejected

You've Been Accepted

The letter should be personal (it's always nice if the admissions office spells your name correctly), congratulating you on your successful application and welcoming you to enroll at the college. But that's not all the letter will say. There's always a little stinger near the end, a conditional clause attached to the acceptance. It will read something like

> *This invitation to become a member of the incoming freshman class is contingent upon your maintaining an honorable academic record, as determined by your final transcript.*

In other words, the pressure's still on. Just because you've got your ticket of admission doesn't mean that you can coast from here on in. Your college will be taking a look at your final grade-point average and your class ranking. If there's anything the admissions office doesn't want to see, it's a steep drop in academic performance in your senior year.

Such a decline could trigger any number of unpleasant reactions by the college. Among these could be

- requiring you to enroll in summer school as a new condition for admission in the fall;
- requiring you to take basic courses at the college level (not getting transfer credit for certain high-school classes if you performed poorly in them);
- delaying your admission by a semester;
- withdrawing your acceptance altogether.

Of course, it goes without saying that any serious academic violation (cheating, plagiarism, hacking or otherwise altering grades) will undoubtedly be reported by school authorities to those colleges that have already accepted or are considering accepting the offenders. No college welcomes known cheats and academic swindlers. On the other hand, many colleges may not necessarily care to know about social or moral offenses, no matter how stern a view they may take of such offenses. For instance, our school suspends students who drink alcoholic beverages and expels those who use drugs. But among the colleges and universities to which our graduates go, only the evangelical Christian colleges express any wish to be informed about such disciplinary action.

Also included in your letter of congratulations will be yet another paragraph telling you that the college wants to know your decision soon. In the case of the April 15 notification of Ivy League and other schools, you have until May 1 to decide. If you accept admission, then the college expects a check for something like $200 or even $400 as a non-refundable deposit.

This money holds your place in line and is usually credited toward your first semester's tuition and fees. But if you change your mind and don't end up attending that school, don't expect to get your money back.

SOME GOOD NEWS ABOUT ACCEPTANCE AND FINANCIAL AID

In almost every instance, if you're accepted and you need financial assistance, the college intends to make it possible for you to attend. If your application indicated a need for financial aid, your letter of acceptance may be accompanied by additional forms for your parents to complete. The college's financial-aid officers use these forms to determine the amount of your grant.

Of course, if you didn't ask for financial aid in your original application, the college is assuming that you and your family will cover all expenses and has accepted you on that basis. Unless your family's circumstances have changed radically in the few months since you applied (due to death or divorce or the collapse of the family business), the college won't be particularly happy to learn that now you've decided that you need financial aid.

When all your family's financial information has been submitted to and processed by the college, you'll be sent an offer of financial aid. In some unusual instances, it may consist of an outright subsidy covering all your expenses—tuition, fees, room and board, even books. This would be the kind of grant reserved for brilliant scholars or seven-foot-tall basketball stars. Most often, however, colleges offer financial aid in smaller packages and from a variety of sources.

The final form you receive may look something like this (though the figures won't mirror those you see here):

Cost per Semester		Source of Payment and Aid	
Tuition	$3900	Parents' contribution	$2050
Fees	$200	Student's summer job	1000
Room	$1050	College grant	1250
Board	$1300	Work/study program	510
Books	$350	Stafford Loan program	1250
Living Expenses	$435	Perkins Loan program	890
Transportation	$250	Pell Grant	535
Total Cost	$7485	Total Payment and Aid	$7485

Under the "Cost per Semester" heading, the college will indicate its charges and its estimates of a student's personal expenses. Under "Source of Aid," the college will indicate its offered and recommended means of meeting its costs. The college will list whatever funds are available through federal-aid programs, depending on current legislation and qualifying standards. These Pell Grants (named for Senator Claiborne Pell of Rhode Island) support hundreds of thousands of college students.

The college may also offer limited proceeds from an endowed scholarship fund, which is a sum of money given to the college and invested so that the interest earned can be distributed to students like you.

Endowment funds generally bear the name of the donor or person in whose memory the funds were donated, like these:

Cora Blanche Fricker Scholarship	$600.00
Napoleon Bibeau Foundation	750.00
Olsen Sisters Trust	1,000.00

You won't necessarily recognize the names of your benefactors; they aren't all as famous as Andrew Carnegie or John D. Rockefeller. Some of the grants may be rather small—just a few hundred dollars. But each of them, however large or small, reflects generosity and can help cover your educational expenses.

Your college may also be able to apply funds from a particular scholarship fund for which you qualify because of your parents' military experience or their employment: Your notice may read something like this:

Veterans of Foreign Wars Fund	$1,500.00
United Auto Workers Scholarship	800.00
GTE Employees' Matching Fund	400.00
New York State Employees' Grant	250.00

Under federal regulations, you may qualify for a special grant available only to members of an ethnic or racial minority; if you're a woman interested in a field of study dominated by men, such as engineering or aviation, you might find funds available from Affirmative Action/Equal Opportunity appropriations.

The aid you receive may come from unlikely sources. Ellyn was surprised to discover that part of her financial aid for her junior and senior years at Chapel Hill came from the accumulated interest on unclaimed bank accounts in the State of North Carolina. She had nothing to do with obtaining those funds; people had just let their bank accounts become inactive, and after a certain legal period, those funds reverted to the state for use in its university's financial aid program.

In addition to noting what kind of scholarship or grant money you may be eligible for, the college will specify other sources for obtaining money to be applied to your college costs. These may include a student employment program whereby the college guarantees you a job related in some way to your academic interests; or you may be given a menial task such as bussing trays of dirty dishes in the cafeteria or making rounds as a member of the campus security force. In any case, the college will probably estimate your working up to ten hours per week and applying most of what you earn toward your college bills.

Finally, the college will estimate two essential factors:

- how much you will earn in summer jobs;
- how much your family is expected to contribute.

These two sums combined will probably assume the greatest burden for paying your college costs.

There's no getting around it: Your college expects you to be gainfully employed each summer, earning as much as you can toward the next year's tuition and other bills. As for your parents, the college expects them to go into debt, if necessary, to pay for your education. Typically, your family is expected to borrow 50 percent or more of the cost of your college education. The college may or may not offer you and them a direct loan; if not, the college may expect your family to apply for a loan from a local bank or savings institution. Such loans are usually available at minimal interest; repayment starts upon completion of your education and extends over a five-to-ten-year period. It's important that this loan be repaid. If it isn't, it can haunt your credit record for years to come and even show up when you apply for a job or a driver's license in a different state.

Supposing what the college offers isn't enough? Suppose that even with a loan from the bank, the money's just not there? If this happens, we urge you to go back to the college's financial aid office and present your case. There's not an unlimited reservoir of funds stashed away somewhere in the college's vaults, but an institution has resources that individuals don't have. If the college wants you, really wants you, it will find the money you need.

If your appeal is turned down, or even the additional money granted isn't enough, then you have no alternative but to select a less costly form of college education:

- a work/study opportunity like that offered by North-eastern University in Boston;
- an ROTC, NROTC, or other officers' training program funded by a branch of the military and requiring a commitment to military service following your graduation;
- a combination of part-time work and part-time study at a public university or community college near your home.

You've Been Put on a Waiting List or Have to Wait for Another Deferred Decision

Agonizing as it might be, your waiting could be just beginning. You may be notified that the college you most want to attend has placed your name on its waiting list or has decided to offer you admission in the spring semester rather than in the fall. What do you do?

If it's your first choice that's put you on hold, you have a dilemma. It's even tougher if you're informed about the waiting list after April 15, when everybody's pressing you for a decision. While you certainly don't want to wait indefinitely for your first choice to make up its mind, acting hastily could affect your standing with your second choice, which has accepted you.

Here are some options:

1. WRITE OFF YOUR FIRST CHOICE AND GLADLY ACCEPT YOUR SECOND CHOICE.

This way you're not left hanging; you're in charge of the decision-making timetable.

2. BE PATIENT AND WAIT IT OUT.

How long will you have to wait? Maybe until May 15—make that June 1, if you must know. Colleges tend to be tardy about informing wait-listed applicants. Be sure to write back and tell your first choice that you wish to remain on the active waiting list. If they don't hear from you, they may assume that you're no longer interested.

3. PAY YOUR DEPOSIT AT YOUR SECOND CHOICE BUT KEEP YOUR NAME ON THE WAITING LIST OF YOUR FIRST CHOICE.

This way you keep both your options open: to be accepted at your first choice or to go where you've already been accepted. But you've also made the decision to forfeit your deposit at your second choice if you get into your first choice.

If, when you finally hear from your first choice, the news is good, do the considerate thing and notify your second choice that you won't be enrolling. Remember, they probably have a waiting list too, and some other senior is probably waiting just like you were, hoping to hear that there's a place for him. Your good news can become his good news too.

Your school counselor and your parents and friends can help you sort out these decisions.

You've Been Rejected

"Thanks, but no thanks," says your letter. Of course, there's bound to be a few elaborate sentences intended to soften the impact:

> *An unusually large number of applications from the most capable pool of candidates has made it impossible for us to grant admission to all who qualified. Unhappily, you are among those we must decline to accept . . .*

Whatever the phrasing, the effect is the same. You've been turned away at the gate.

This is a devastating moment for some students—but it's even harder for some parents. Sometimes they call the admissions officer and complain. "You've ruined my daughter's life!" they scream—which isn't true. "It's not fair!" they shout. "My son's best friend was accepted, and he had lower SAT scores. How dare you reject my son!" The admissions officer didn't "dare" to do it—he or she said no with difficulty, and certainly without malicious intent. Parental reactions like this over-simplify the application process. It's a process that presumes both selection and rejection, with many factors—including both objective information and subjective interpretation of that information—combining to make up the mix that finally results in a decision by the admissions team. Those comparative SAT scores may have been only a minor part of the decision-making.

How you react to a rejection, if it comes, depends on several factors:

- how insistently you want to pursue and plead with the college admissions department to reverse its decision;
- how convinced you are that this is the only college for you;
- how confident you are that your school counselor can use his or her influence to get you a second hearing;
- how persuasive you think you or your parents can be in pleading your case with the college;

- how willing you are to accept this decision as God's providence rather than as some human blunder or failure.

Of course, you can decide to go to war. You can demand another chance. You can make phone calls and have other people call on your behalf. You can try tears, and you can try selling yourself as a diamond in the rough who's somehow been overlooked. An argument can be made for refusing to accept the college's rejection without a protest.

Or you can take it all in stride and move along. We think, generally speaking, that that's the classy thing to do.

ACCEPTANCE IS A TWO-WAY STREET

Assuming you've heard positively from more than one college, you'll have only a brief time to think about your final decision. Those selective colleges that notify you on April 15 want an answer by May 1.

But you've got some leeway here, especially if you're waiting for a final word on financial aid. We advise you to respond immediately, by phone or letter, to the person who signed your letter of acceptance, informing the college of your delight in being accepted but also stating that you can't issue a formal letter of your own until you know the details of each college's financial offer.

Remember, acceptance works both ways. First the colleges accept you, then you accept one of them. When you have in hand your checklist of pros and cons for each of your colleges, and the final financial-aid offers or other strategies to pay for your education, you're ready to make the first truly major decision of your life. Others will follow, but this one has the potential to shape much of the rest of your life.

Make your decision

- carefully
- prayerfully
- share-fully

Decide Carefully

Take into account all those factors we've discussed. Don't go against your own best inclinations; don't be a pushover. If you still have unanswered questions about a college and its offerings, call the admissions office or the particular department you need to know more about and tell somebody that your decision hinges on getting satisfactory answers to your questions. You'll probably get what you're looking for.

Decide Prayerfully

You know where we stand on religious concerns. We believe that God hears and answers prayer, especially the prayer for guidance. The Bible records how Solomon as a young man set us all a good example when he asked God for "a discerning heart" (1 Kings 3:9) to make wise decisions. Don't be ashamed to be as wise as Solomon and ask God to help you make your choice.

Decide Share-fully

Don't exclude your parents from your decision-making. Count them in as partners. In the long run, of course, it's best if the final decision is yours; after all, *you* rather than your parents are enrolling in whichever college is chosen. Even so, your parents do have a vested interest in your well-being and in the choice you make. So take their advice seriously, even if it seems just a bit heavy-handed. We're sure they mean well.

We remember going through those anxious days with our own children. For instance, after Don had narrowed his choices to Missouri, North Carolina, Pennsylvania, and Wheaton, his parents insisted that he draw up a checklist. They worked with him all one Sunday afternoon in late April while he struggled to eliminate two of the four. That evening, after Don and his folks prayed together, his folks left him alone to come to his own choice between the Southern university and the Midwestern college; his own choice between the public, secular institution and the evangelical Christian institution; his own choice between living in an environment sometimes hostile to his own professed faith and upbringing or living in an environment more often compatible with his faith and homelife; his own choice of athletic participation against either NCAA Division I competition or Division III opponents; his own choice between academic study in a university environment (with some courses taught by graduate students) and academic study in a college environment in which experienced professors teach at every level. His *own* choice.

Don's parents wanted him to make that choice—carefully, prayerfully, and with shared responsibility—because they love him.

Most parents want what's best for their children. Letting go and letting you make a wise choice helps send you on your way toward maturity.

CHAPTER 7

Coping in Advance: Preparing for Social and Emotional Adjustment

The motto of the Boy Scouts of America has always been "Be Prepared." This could also be the motto for every college freshman.

We've already talked about academic preparation. You get your high-school courses lined up properly, go to classes regularly, do your best work in those classes, take the right admissions tests, fill out the application forms, and mail them early enough to be considered for acceptance. But preparing for college isn't quite as mechanical as that—it means preparing for a big adjustment.

Some adjustments are natural and easily accepted. For instance, we adjust to the annual cycle of the seasons by changing what we wear. If a new supermarket opens close to your home and your mother decides to shop there instead of at your old grocery store, she soon adjusts to the differences between the familiar store and the new one. In school we adjust to the change from one grade level to another.

But change that involves personal relationships can be more stressful. So transferring from one school to another is harder than merely advancing a grade in the same school. Friends and acquaintances may not be making that same change with you, and as they leave you to go their own way, the adjustment that follows is somewhat painful. That's why, on such a seemingly joyful day as high-school commencement, you and your friends, as well as your parents, have mixed emotions—you're happy and sad at the same time.

Families also experience changes, some less dramatic than others, but all carrying the potential for stress—a move from one city to another, a change in economic circumstances, a change in marital stability and family life, a change brought about by sickness or death. Even now, some of you reading this book are going through one or more of these changes. You know what we're talking about.

By deciding to attend college, you've chosen to make some perfectly normal changes in your life. But unless you prepare for them, you could find them overwhelming.

WHAT'S AHEAD?

One of the best ways to help you cope with coming change is to investigate the kinds of changes you'll probably face:

- lifestyle changes
- social changes
- emotional changes
- academic changes

We're going to talk about academic changes in the next chapter. In this chapter we want to concentrate on these first three kinds of change you can expect.

Surviving Lifestyle Changes

Up until now, you've probably enjoyed a life that's been fairly private and stable, marked by a regular routine. You've probably lived in your own house or apartment with only the other members of your immediate family present, except for occasional visits by relatives. It could be that you've lived in your town or city for five or ten years; maybe you've never lived anywhere else, not even in another house. When you hear the word "home," you have only one place in mind: you automatically think of a weathered shingle house on Cedar Street or an apartment building near the park.

You're comfortable in your home, especially in your own bedroom, where you have all your treasures on display or stored in the back of your closet. Your walls are filled with class photos, a couple of certificates to show that you once were an expert marksman in summer camp or passed your Red Cross lifesaving course, pennants and posters from places you've visited, maybe a couple of concert souvenirs. Around your desk are books you've never gotten around to reading (but they fill the shelves nicely), records, and tapes. You might have your own stereo system.

This is your castle, your private office, your place for personal reflection and, when necessary, recuperation from the stress of living. If you have a good relationship with your family, you hardly ever need to shut the door because they respect your privacy—at least, most of the time.

Your other favorite room in the house is the kitchen, where your mom keeps the cupboards and the refrigerator stocked with your favorite foods and drinks. Anytime you want you can go down to the kitchen and find something good to eat.

Then there's the family room or den, where most of the TV-watching goes on—not 24 hours a day, but pretty often. Everybody in the family has a say in choosing what gets watched (although Mom and Dad have veto power), and there's a second set in the basement to resolve most conflicts. The VCR gets a lot of use on the weekends.

Ideally, you're in a relaxed situation in which each member of the household thoughtfully shares the common living areas and enjoys a zone of quiet and privacy.

Be prepared for a big change when you go to college.

The first and probably the biggest adjustment you'll have to make to college living will involve your living arrangements. Most colleges and universities require entering freshmen—except commuters—to live on campus. You can expect to live in a freshman dorm. In fact, as you may learn to your later pain, dormitory space is generally limited, and there's no guarantee that you'll have a room after your sophomore year. To keep space available for all freshmen, many colleges simply conduct a lottery for a few rooms for upperclassmen; if you lose, you're on your own, and you'll have to find a room or share an apartment somewhere off campus.

And the quality of the space probably won't be what you're used to, either. The building itself may be an old, ivy-covered relic from the nineteenth century; if it is, it won't have air conditioning, and the heating system will clank and grind like an army tank. Or the building may be a modern high-rise, in which case you'll spend half your first semester waiting for an elevator to take you to the twelfth floor.

Your assigned room won't be anything like your room at home. Expect it to be small—very small. Its walls will probably be painted a sick beige and will be scarred from the war between last year's occupants. There'll be two single beds or a bunk bed, with mattresses either too soft or too hard for your preference, two tiny bureaus or dressers (mirrors aren't necessarily included), two desks the size of a piano bench and chairs that don't match. Assume that closet space will be inadequate. There won't be a rug on the floor or curtains on the single window, and the single ceiling light won't illuminate the gloom, making desk lamps a necessity. However, as you'll discover, the only electrical outlets will be strategically placed to make it impossible to live without a string of extension cords.

Not all college and university accommodations are this spartan. But however few or many basic comforts are provided, you'll be faced with a living situation that will be significantly different from what you're used to.

Sometime during midsummer, your college will have sent you the name and home address of your prospective roommate. In certain situations, make that *roommates*, plural. You may discover that you've been assigned to a triple room, which makes your new adventure twice as challenging. Space will be even tighter and the need for good relationships that much more important. The benefits, of course, are that you start out with two different people—presumably two different temperaments and personalities—instead of only one. On those mornings when one of your roommates may be grouchy, you'll have the other one to talk with. The disadvantages arise if you discover that neither roommate is a person you would have chosen to live with. One would be bad enough, but two. . . !

In some extraordinarily rare instances, you may have been able to arrange to room with a friend. One of our sons, Kevin, lived for three years with Mark, his high-school friend and teammate. They were a wonderfully compatible pair, and their friendship remains strong to this day, years after college. But that's unusual in both respects: first, being able to arrange to room with someone you know and, second, remaining friends after living together. Some friendships can't endure the inevitable strains of rooming together.

The probability is that your roommate will be a stranger, and the biggest adjustment of your life will begin when you read that name and realize that you'll be sharing your living quarters with that person. In many ways it's like marrying someone you've never seen until the ceremony. Of course, many people in other cultures do precisely that and manage to develop mutual respect and, eventually, affection for each other. In the same way, for centuries strangers thrown together as college roommates have gotten to know each other and learned to live in harmony. You probably will too.

In all likelihood, you and your new acquaintance will get along fine and become lifelong friends. It happens all the time. But, just as a couple has to work at a marriage, you'll have to work at achieving harmony and tranquility; you'll have to struggle against being selfish and holding grudges. If you're a believer, you'll have to pray for grace and sometimes for forgiveness.

One way to make your first meeting a little less of a strain would be to call in advance—soon after you receive each other's name—and introduce yourself over the phone, or write a friendly note and send a photo. You might want to discuss what the two of you could contribute to make dorm life more bearable. For instance, would a mini-refrigerator be a useful convenience? If so, how about sharing the cost of renting one? Would a sofa fit? If so, who'll be responsible for lugging it up to the room? Are aesthetics important? Would you like to have a pair of drapes or curtains with matching bedspreads, or don't you care if you're mixing stripes with paisleys or a down comforter with a traditional chenille bedspread?

GIVING UP IN ORDER TO GAIN

College is meant to be a time for growth, for emerging from the isolation and protection of your family to face the world. College administrators will tell you that one of the most broadening experiences you can have comes from learning about human nature by living with strangers who become friends.

The only way to move from being strangers toward becoming friends is by *compromise,* with each of you agreeing to give up certain things in order to achieve others. We're not talking about moral issues here—simply the kind of compromise that leads to mutual understanding and goodwill. Think of it as something like the rules of the road: I'll watch out for the other driver's safety and my own by respecting both our rights to drive on the same highway; I'll expect the other driver to do likewise. In much the same way, you'll compromise on your living arrangements to achieve a peaceful environment.

For instance, you'll divide up the furniture and limited common space. It may take some hard-nosed bargaining to achieve a fair distribution of living space and its comforts, especially if either you or your roommate is used to luxury. But reason can usually prevail. Take Ellyn's situation. When she arrived at school for her sophomore year and checked into her dorm room, she found a freshman named Lisa whose mother had taken over both closets and both dressers. Ellyn's mother was outraged, but Ellyn easily informed Lisa that they'd be sharing the room and its furnishings, so she'd better decide which clothes would fit into the single closet and dresser that would be hers and which would have to go back home.

Remember, adjusting to dorm life is just as hard on your roommate as it is on you. Both of you have been accustomed to arranging your bedroom the way you want it. Now you have to find an arrangement that suits both your tastes. Your college may permit you to repaint the room in any color you choose, and you'll have to find one that both of you like. You'll find out that there are ingenious ways to arrange and decorate the room; you'll learn a lot by watching what other dorm residents do.

Both you and your roommate will be giving up privacy. You may be a very shy person; you may have felt ill at ease about getting dressed for gym class in your school locker room. Now you're going to be dressing and undressing in your own dorm room, and a lot of the time somebody else is going to be there. Maybe you won't feel so awkward if you remember that, at first, your roommate will be a little uncomfortable too. Gradually you'll both grow less self-conscious.

Like Felix and Oscar in Neil Simon's play *The Odd Couple*, the two of you may discover that you have different standards of tidiness. You may be accustomed to dropping your under-wear on the floor, while your roommate folds his slacks on the crease and places them carefully on a clothes hanger. Or vice versa: you may have learned to make up your bed so tightly that a dime bounces off the covers, while your roommate never even bothers to rearrange the pillow, sheets, and blankets. You may not want to live in a room littered with stacks of empty pizza boxes and crushed Pepsi cans. On the other hand, your roommate may drive you crazy with her constant mopping-up operations every time she sees a fleck of dust.

Can you learn to handle it?

You may dislike the smell of your roommate's aftershave or even be allergic to your roommate's favorite cologne or hairspray. You may be used to studying in complete silence, while your roommate can't read a book without the stereo blaring. Or you may be a "Tonight Show" fanatic, so you brought your own TV set so you don't miss a single show, but your roommate expects the room to be as silent as a tomb when he/she studies. You may have come to college to learn and study and supposed that everyone else came for the same reason; to your surprise, you find that your roommate and most of her friends are there to party.

You may be a morning person, but because your roommate is a night owl and keeps your room lit up until long after midnight, you have to tiptoe around in the morning so you don't disturb her. Your roommate may feel that what's yours is hers and vice versa, so that you constantly see her wearing your clothes on campus. Or your roommate may have a forgetful streak and never seem to have remembered his key at two o'clock in the morning. Or your roommate may borrow small amounts of money and neglect to repay you.

How much would any of these things annoy you? Can you learn to talk out these difficulties without getting into major arguments?

But there could be more serious problems. You may object to the posters your roommate wants to put up, or the loud music she likes, or the friends he invites over as if he owns your room, or her contempt for college rules and the law in general.

He may be a nice guy but have a foul mouth. She may be an atheist and find it hard to believe that she shares a room with someone who reads the Bible every day. Or maybe you're the atheist and she's the Bible reader. And what if you come back to the dorm and find your room occupied temporarily—or for the night—by your roommate's fellow drug-users or current lover?

Is there a chance for compromise, or is this a doomed situation?

That's tough to decide. Every instance is different, and we're not here to tell you what's absolute. In certain cases, it's best to grit your teeth and endure; in others, you may have no option but to find other housing. Or you may have to demand your rights and stick by them. The one year that Kevin didn't room with his friend Mark was the worst year he spent at the university. His roommate, Reese, was a slob. Apparently he never took a shower, and he lived and slept in the same warm-up suit all year. Not surprisingly, he smelled, and his body odor permeated the room. Kevin kept a window fan on constantly to drive out the stench. Reese also drank too much on weekends. Kevin had legitimate complaints against Reese, but his appeals to the university housing authority went unanswered. As an in-state resident, Reese had priority over Kevin, who was an out-of-state complainant. Kevin reached his limit of tolerance on the spring night that Reese staggered into the room and in the dark stood at his own bed urinating on his pillow. Kevin literally threw Reese and his belongings out of the room for good, refusing to let him come back. The other residents in nearby rooms supported him, and the situation was resolved only by that unhappy circumstance.

This is a scenario more likely to occur at a large university. At many of the smaller colleges, dorm life is treated as a significant part of the college experience; there are well-trained residence-hall supervisors (sometimes young faculty or graduate students) who have assistants, usually carefully selected upperclassmen. At these colleges, dormitory life becomes *community* life. Kevin and his wife Kimberly know this side of the coin too, having spent two years as residence-hall directors at Gordon College, an evangelical college in Massachusetts, where they lived in apartments next to students' rooms.

In the atmosphere of a small college, students are more likely to find companionship and counsel, as well as encouragement—and, when necessary, reprimand—from caring young adults near enough to their own age to understand what it's like to be away from home. Of course, in every college dorm—even at a small Christian college—there may be instances of anti-social and even illegal behavior. But chances are that someone in charge, if he or she is properly informed, will be able to do something about it.

Few large-scale universities can live up to such a standard. They all have their residence-hall directors and assistants, but a high-rise dorm in which occupants share few of the same values simply can't be as wholesome an environment as the smaller college dorm. So rules and even laws are casually overlooked. In fact, all too often the resident adviser's motto in a university dorm is "Don't bother me and I won't bother you."

SHARING A COMMON FAITH

Of course, it's easier to avoid the more serious problems if you and your roommate share a common faith and set of values. When Ellyn was a freshman, her roommate, Dora, was a sophomore. Dora was a rural country girl, while Ellyn was cosmopolitan by comparison, someone from New York who had traveled around the world. Dora was black and Ellyn was white, and neither of them had lived with someone of a different race. Both were Christians, but while Ellyn was an Episcopalian, Dora was from a Pentecostal church; each knew a different way of worshiping and praising God. On the surface, these two didn't have much to share. But they had at least this much in common: they both recognized the same God and their need for prayer and Bible reading. They made time for sharing devotions together, and they learned to respect each other.

Surviving Social Changes

Get ready for some major adjustments in your social life. For one thing, chances are you'll be spending a lot more time with a lot more people than you did previously. Of course, there are always exceptions. You may live in New York or Chicago or Los Angeles and be a high-school student at one of the huge public schools in your city, and you may choose to attend a tiny college in the farm belt—in which case your world would seem to shrink. But for most college-bound teenagers, even if the college town or city is small by hometown standards, the college or university itself is often much larger and certainly more spread out than their high schools.

So how do you get to know people and have them get to know you? As you start this process, it's helpful to remember the difference between acquaintances and friends. All of us have lots of acquaintances: classmates, teammates, people we recognize and nod to in passing. Some we know only by reputation; others we'd choose to share a meal with or even arrange to ride with at Thanksgiving. But they're really only acquaintances.

Friends, on the other hand, are something special. By definition, friends are loyal, friends are loving, friends will live and die for each other. Popularity has almost nothing to do with friendship. Popular people have numerous acquaintances, lots of companions, but friends are rare.

We encourage you to make as many friends as you can. But be aware that you'll probably consider yourself fortunate if, when you graduate from college, you can name a handful of true friends.

BE FRIENDLY

How do you go about making friends, real friends, the kind who won't let you down or be a bad influence on you?

Even if you haven't been the gregarious type in high school, in college you're starting over in a new environment. So is almost everyone else you'll meet during the first few days of freshman orientation. When you arrive at your campus and discover that your room is in the belltower of Old Main—four flights up a curving stairway—you and especially your dad will appreciate any help you can get with your boxes and suitcases. So if an upperclassman wearing an orientation T-shirt approaches you and asks if he can lend a hand, welcome his help. Do the same with anyone else who approaches you. Then, when you're settled in your room, your folks are gone, and you're getting familiar with the campus, offer to help some later-arriving newcomer. You'll make an acquaintance, maybe even a friend.

You'll start meeting people everywhere, every time you leave your dorm. More people, starting with long lines at registration tables during the opening days of the term. More people standing in line—in the student union waiting to have pictures taken for their student ID cards, in the cafeteria waiting for lunch, in the bookstores waiting to pay for textbooks and supplies, in the residence hall waiting for mailbox keys, in the gym waiting for locker assignments. Everywhere, lines of people waiting.

Get used to waiting a lot. And while you're standing there, waiting for the line to move, you've got a great chance to get acquainted with people around you who are doing just what you're doing.

Make small talk—about how slow the line is moving, about how awful the food is, about how expensive the textbooks are and how you'll never get through Psychology 101 . . . You don't need to get into your life's history, or the fact that you're there on a full academic scholarship. Just be casually friendly.

You'll find people you feel comfortable and natural with. This is affinity, which occurs in relationships that complement both parties and bring out the best in each. You'll meet quiet, solid people you could trust with your life; you'll meet happy-go-lucky types always ready with a joke; you'll meet Good Samaritans who can't do enough for others. You'll also meet loudmouths and boasters, flirts of both sexes, schemers and connivers, nerds and jocks, political types and fraternity types, budding yuppies and high-school homecoming queens with dreams of new worlds to conquer. Get to know better those who seem most natural and unaffected, those least impressed with themselves. You'll find a friend or two among that group.

You'll also make acquaintances and perhaps find friends in the dorms, in your classes, in the library—and in extra-curricular groups. Early in the semester each campus organization will hold a welcoming meeting. As we've already discussed, even the varsity teams will hold tryouts for "walk-on" athletes, those who haven't been recruited and who aren't receiving financial grants for their athletic participation. Be sure to find out about these opportunities, especially since some of them will be picnics or cookouts. They really are open to everyone.

And keep in mind that college publications such as the newspaper and the yearbook are looking for writers and photographers; musical groups are looking for singers and instrumentalists; drama groups are looking for stagehands and ushers and lighting engineers as much as actors. Just remember to be modest about your high-school accomplishments. As a freshman you'll have to take some starting positions, to work your way in and up.

You may also want to attend the meetings of campus groups such as Inter-Varsity Christian Fellowship, Campus Crusade for Christ, Navigators, or Fellowship of Christian Athletes. (To find out how to get information about them, see Chapter Eleven.) If you're a believer, you'll probably find people with whom you have something in common at these meetings. You can probably count on meeting friendly people at the local church of your denomination, too.

Surviving the Social Pressures

Pressure comes in different forms:

- pressure to conform (peer pressure);
- pressure to spend your time doing something other than studying (which is why you enrolled in college);
- pressure to spend more money than you have on clothes or entertainment or worse (which leads to begging, borrowing, or worse).

At first you'll probably find adequate fulfillment in the handful of friendships you're developing. But sooner or later some of your friends may begin to drift away from you, or you'll lose interest in them, one by one, and move on to a new set of friends. It happens quite naturally. One of them discovers love and another decides to go the fraternity or sorority route (we'll discuss this in Chapter Nine); another joins a club that takes up all his time; another discovers that she has to take a part-time job to make ends meet. You may learn that you need to spend more time with the books than some of your more brilliant (or less dedicated) friends do. Or you may simply grow tired of their idea of fun and look for other friends. And when you're looking for new relationships, peer pressure can mount.

By now you know that there's no pressure quite like peer pressure. Sometimes peer pressure can be a positive influence. Say your roommate and some friends are going to a political rally or a lecture by a famous scholar or a Fellowship of Christian Athletes meeting. Ordinarily you'd stay at the dorm and watch MTV, but you yield to their cajoling and go with them. That's positive peer pressure.

Negative peer pressure tells you, "Never mind the quiz tomorrow. The prof will probably forget he announced it. Come with us to the basketball game." So, foolishly, you go along, and the next day the professor gives the announced quiz and you get an F. All because you tried to please other people.

BE YOURSELF

Misusing your time and spending your money thriftlessly are also related to trying to please other people. There's really only one solution to surviving the social pressures, and that's to assert whatever strength of character you possess, to be yourself.

EAT REGULARLY AND WELL

You'll make other companions in the cafeteria or at the nearby off-campus restaurants, the favorite haunts of hungry students late at night and on the weekends. Remember that a companion is someone with whom you break bread—someone with whom you feel at home while you sit at the table and talk. And a companion with whom you frequently share a meal may become a friend. But while your friendship is important, so is what and when you eat. Maybe you don't know much about diet and nutrition; maybe you haven't had a lot of experience with cafeteria-style eating; maybe you're already addicted to nachos and Twinkies and Big Macs. If so, you need to realize that you can deprive your system of its needed fuel by filling your stomach with junk while your blood, muscles, and bones cry out for real nutrition.

It's essential that you establish regular and healthy eating habits right from the start. True, it's unlikely that the food at college (prepared by a local chef or by a food-service organization like Marriott or Saga) will appeal to you in quite the same way that Mom's home-cooked meals do, but two other things are also true: the college food won't hurt you, but not eating properly and regularly will.

The first temptation is going to be to sleep in so late that you don't have time for a decent breakfast. Let's say your first class is at 8:00 o'clock. You set the alarm for 7:30, rush through getting showered and dressed, and on the run from the dorm to class grab a package of cheese crackers (with imitation cheese-flavored spread) from the dispensing machine in the Student Union building. These give you some quick energy but little else that's good for you. There's virtually no nutritional value in these crackers, and they're not going to give you the long-term energy you need. You've left yourself vulnerable to hunger and fatigue just because you didn't allow time for the day's most important meal— the hearty breakfast every good nutritionist recommends.

Or maybe you decide that, since you have an hour off in mid-morning, you'll stop at the Union snack bar to get a fried egg on a bagel at 10:15. Not good enough. All you get is a lot of cholesterol, grease, and dough, with a little protein fighting against overwhelming odds.

What you need to do is discipline yourself to allow time for proper meals at regular times. And it's possible to choose as well in the cafeteria line as you did in the registration line. Here are some hints:

1. *Know how much your food-service plan entitles you to eat, then eat less.*

Most college food services offer an open, all-you-can-eat policy, often supplying a lot of "filler" food. Avoid falling into the quantity trap that's set for you. Limit yourself to one entree even if you can have both. Take one dessert instead of two. Even if you can have seconds and thirds, you'll feel better— and look better—if you eat in moderation.

2. Read the menu and be selective.

Pick and choose among the main courses. Stay away from "mystery meat," greasy gravies, and space-age substitutes for real food like freeze-dried bacon bits that might look good but taste like plastic wrap.

3. Plan your day's nutrition to include each of the four major food groups.

First, include *grains:* cereals (but not the sugar-coated kind), breads, and pasta—macaroni, spaghetti, noodles, ravioli, and lasagna in modest portions. Second, include *milk and dairy products,* preferably low-fat (products with 2 percent milk fat or less), definitely not with chocolate added and definitely not the processed products imitating dairy foods (these tend to be very high in fat). Third, include *meat, fish, and chicken,* with as little red meat (fatty beef especially) as possible. Cut down on hamburgers. (Autopsies on young American soldiers in Vietnam revealed levels of cholesterol once typical of middle-aged and older men. Experts blame the soldiers' heavy intake of fast-food hamburgers.) While you're at it, avoid eating the skin on chicken and turkey (very fatty). Have fish whenever possible (preferably broiled, not fried). Also avoid luncheon meats and the all-American hotdog, which is nothing more than pork scraps from the slaughterhouse floor stuffed into a tube. Fourth, include lots of *fruits and vegetables,* preferably raw or at most lightly cooked so that the vitamins haven't been boiled away.

4. Load up at the salad bar.

You may not like the typical salad. But most college cafeterias have salad bars that go well beyond lettuce and tomatoes. Unfortunately, many food-service agencies use preservatives to keep their salad fixings looking fresh, but that doesn't cancel the value of these foods. For maximum nutritional benefit, choose the raw broccoli and cauliflower, the spinach leaves and carrot sticks, the seeds and fruit and cottage cheese— what's freshest and closest to its natural state. Avoid most of the prepared salads (they're full of oil and mayonnaise), and go easy on the salad dressings (very fatty).

5. Drink lots of water, and don't become a caffeine addict.

The old family doctor was right: eight glasses of water a day will keep the body's plumbing properly functioning and purified. Coffee, tea, and many commercial beverages are temporary stimulants whose effect wears off and leaves you just as thirsty as you were before. Because they contain caffeine, they actually dehydrate you rather than provide your body with the fluid it needs. Besides that, too much caffeine can make you jumpy, and has been linked to physical problems like kidney stones. (Excessive drinking of iced tea, a favorite in the South, is being blamed for the high incidence of kidney stones in that region.)

In time you may discover alternatives to the college food service. For instance, if, as an upperclassman, you're forced out of the dormitory and find yourself sharing an apartment or renting a single room somewhere off-campus, you'll probably find yourself cooking your own meals, whether by stove or microwave. You may even learn how to entertain for dinner with real china and polished silver instead of paper plates and plastic forks. Enjoy being your own chef. There's no shame in knowing how to cook for yourself.

EXERCISE, RECREATION, AND REST

More and more colleges are coming to realize the importance of providing an alternative to student isolation in the dorm room or passive "couch potato" large-screen TV watching in the lounge or student union. Educators are recognizing that idle students often get into trouble, and they're starting to do something about it.

Some actions have been overdue and correct abuses too long permitted by lax administrators. For instance, at the State University of New York at Stony Brook, one of the current president's first acts was to close the bars selling alcoholic beverages in each dormitory complex.

Other actions reflect renewed perceptions about the value of exercise over lethargy. At Wake Forest University, the president has ordered that the TV sets be removed from all dorm lounges. If students feel they must watch TV, they will have to supply their own sets for their own rooms. Wake Forest is converting the TV lounge into a space for exercise equipment and additional quiet study areas.

Deans of student affairs understand that sheer boredom and the weariness of routine sometimes lead to inappropriate and destructive behavior. So Iowa State University, the University of Nebraska, and many other colleges have invested money to construct student recreation centers. There students can work off excess energy during their leisure time doing aerobic exercise, lifting weights, swimming laps, jogging, playing racquetball or tennis or volleyball; for refreshments they can go to the fruit-juice bar and enjoy healthy foods instead of grease-coated hamburgers.

Whether your college has such a facility or not, it will be to your advantage to do some form of regular exercise so that you can work off tension and maintain the energy you need day to day. Perhaps you'll join a dorm touch-football team that plays in the intramural league; maybe you'll keep your gymnastic routine even though you didn't try out for the varsity team. Maybe you'll meet a friend each morning for a jog or a swim or a few cycles on the Universal gym equipment in the training room. Or perhaps you'll just do a nightly set of sit-ups, all by yourself, because you've always done them.

Exercise is important, but so is recreation. You need to take some time off from your studies and your job and other time-bound obligations just to *re-create* your inner well-being. That's part of keeping your life in balance. Remember the advice of the old proverb, "All work and no play makes Jack a dull boy." The same is true for his sister Jill.

Take time for play—not just competitive games, but leisure enjoyment, which will sometimes include *doing nothing*. Yes, we remember what we said about idleness, but spending every afternoon in soap-opera stupor is the unbalanced extreme of enjoying a period of leisure. Take time—or, if necessary, *make* time—to

- take a bike ride along a rural road in spring
- go for a Sunday afternoon stroll with a friend
- visit a sick friend in the college infirmary or town hospital
- support a classmate on one of the varsity teams by attending a home game
- go to a movie you've been wanting to see
- call a high-school friend at another college
- write a letter to your sister or brother or parents
- write a note to your grandparents
- meet someone for a pizza and some conversation
- accept a local church's offer of hospitality to students
- watch your favorite sport on TV
- do nothing and feel good about it
- catch up on your sleep.

If you find that you often have to catch up on your sleep, you might want to re-examine your sleep patterns and calculate how much bed-rest you're actually getting. Ben Franklin was never a freshman at college, so he didn't know how hard it is to achieve the habit of "early to bed and early to rise."

But you know yourself that you can't burn the candle at both ends. Depending on a nap in the middle of the day between classes isn't sufficient; and you certainly can't survive on a succession of all-nighters during exam time and still do your best.

Maybe developing the right sleep habits depends on several factors:

- planning your study schedule to allow for both daily and long-range assignments so that you avoid all-nighters
- making an agreement with your roommate about what study conditions will prevail in your dorm room
- finding those conditions elsewhere—in the library—if necessary
- setting and sticking to a regular time each night to wind down and start getting ready for bed
- keeping the exceptions to that schedule to a minimum so you don't throw off your body clock.

If you find yourself really having trouble sleeping—due to dorm noise or a thoughtless roommate's clatter or the radiator's clanking—consider buying one of those electronic devices which produces "white noise" that will mask these sounds.

If course, if you're losing sleep because you're worried about grades or romance or how things are going at home, you may need to speak to a counselor, pastor, or trusted friend about these problems.

Just as Shakespeare's Macbeth says, "Sleep. . . knits up the raveled sleeve of care." You need your sleep; we all do. Don't neglect it.

Surviving Emotional Changes

College can be filled with good times—so why do some students have a miserable time? Why does one freshman seem completely at home, popular, at ease socially, while another freshman feels lonely, frustrated, unnoticed, a mere face in the crowd? How can one person find so much fulfillment in college life and another be so miserable? How can one young woman thrive and another starve herself to death? How can one young man succeed, while in the same dorm, on the same floor, somebody else is killing himself with liquor or drugs?

There are a lot of good books directly addressing these very questions; in fact, we list several of them in Chapter Eleven. We could write another book just dealing with the subject of emotional changes. That's not our goal here, but we do want to make a few important points.

Every college campus, every college dorm, knows the anxiety of

- loneliness
- homesickness
- depression
- eating disorders, especially anorexia nervosa and bulimia
- substance abuse, especially campus-wide drunkenness, as well as addictions to marijuana, amphetamines, cocaine, and heroin.

It may help you to know that anyone who's away from home and living in a new environment suffers some kind of loneliness for a while; until acquaintances grow into companions, then true friends, everyone feels lonesome in a strange new place. The best remedy for loneliness is sociability. To make friendships, be friendly. Make eye contact with people you pass on campus and say hello. If someone seems eager to extend the greeting by a second sentence or two, stop and talk for a minute. It doesn't have to be a long conversation, just an indication of friendliness. If the person invites you to have a snack and it's convenient for you, why not? Talking over a cup of soup doesn't obligate you further, and you may find a friend. If you're on your way to class, it's easy enough to say no without insulting the person, but set a time to get together tomorrow or next week.

Here are a few more hints about being friendly:

- Try smiling more often. Friendly people appreciate a friendly smile. Scowls and frowns tend to turn others away.
- When someone asks, "How are you?" they don't really expect you to answer by offering a rehash of the fight you had with your boyfriend or the flu you had last week. A brief, cheerful answer is best.
- Don't concentrate all the conversation on yourself and your circumstances. Ask questions that permit the other person to talk about what concerns her or him.
- Don't gossip about other people. The person listening to you as you tear apart someone else's reputation may seem amused by your story, but he or she will know better than to trust you as a friend. The word will get around that you delight in bad-mouthing others, and that's the early death of any friendship.
- Find out what you can do to help others. Surprise someone by offering to help her with some time-consuming chore or by showing up just when he needs a hand in moving his dorm-room furniture.
- Accept help yourself with a grateful spirit.
- Even if you had a reputation as a loner in high school, recognize that part of maturing into a responsible adult means learning personal interdependence: how to meet and respond to other people, how to earn mutual respect and confidence, how to become a trusted friend, how to love and be loved.

If you've known any degree of happiness at home, being separated from family and comfortable surroundings is bound to bring on feelings of homesickness. But, like loneliness, homesickness has its cure. We think the best antidote for homesickness is *joy*.

Think about why you're away from home: Because you're going to college. Because people are sacrificing to pay the college bills. Because people care about your present and future. Because you're preparing for a productive life of service and caring for others. These are cause for joy, for positive feelings that can counter homesickness.

Sometimes college students end up suffering from depression—the constant state of morose and negative attitudes. The symptoms of depression include reduced energy and activity, withdrawal from social contact, sleep disturbances (wakefulness and the inability to go back to sleep), poor concentration, a sense of helplessness, a tendency toward self-accusation and blame, and deep feelings of inferiority. Sometimes severe loneliness and extreme homesickness may eventually lead to depression.

But depression can be caused by other things, too. Maybe you've gotten bad news from home—your parents' marriage is rocky, your favorite uncle is seriously ill, your dog has died. A prolonged case of mononucleosis or other communicable illness can lead to depression, as can the collapse of a romance, academic failure, getting cut from the team or the band or the choir, being rejected by a fraternity or sorority, or any other disappointment. Keeping crazy hours and depriving your body and mind of sufficient sleep can lead to depression, as can robbing your system of nourishing food.

In fact, the single greatest cause of depression may be the anxiety you generate within yourself. It's like a poison clogging your bloodstream with negative thoughts: "You're no good. You can't make it. You don't belong here. Nobody likes you." And so on.

Depression is a serious affliction, and sometimes a deceptive one: it doesn't always show itself in sour expressions and fits of tears. Sometimes the victim of depression seems cheerful and lighthearted to everyone else, but inside she knows the shallowness of those appearances. The fact is, depression can turn into suicidal intent. It needs to be addressed by the campus health service and student-affairs counselors. If you think you may be suffering from depression, get help—it's the healthy thing to do. If you know someone who you think is depressed, urge them to get help.

As for eating disorders and substance abuse, these too are serious because of their potentially lethal effects. If someone you care about needs help, don't be ashamed to get that help. A drunk's best friend isn't the person who lets the drunk drive home; it's the guy who takes his car keys away from him. In the same way, an anorexic's best friend, a bulimic's best friend, and a cocaine user's best friend is the person who says, "I'm reporting you to somebody who can see that you get help."

If you need help, don't be too proud to accept it.

A Note to the World Traveler

Perhaps the college student who faces the toughest adjustment is the world traveler who arrives in the United States with an American passport and a foreign orientation. Maybe you're the son of a member of the diplomatic corps, and you've spent most of your life in Central America. Maybe you're the daughter of Christian missionaries, and you've just graduated from Rift Valley Academy in Kenya or Morrison Academy in Taiwan or Faith Academy in the Philippines. Maybe you're an Army brat, and you really don't have any idea of *home* except the latest PX.

We know kids like you. Three of our daughters were missionaries' kids (MK's) who came "home" to an America they hardly knew and a culture alien to them. Cindy went off to college worried that maybe her clothes looked funny or she didn't know the current slang. She was so homesick for Africa and her family that she'd go to a shower stall, turn on the water, and just sit there sobbing—she didn't want anyone to see or hear her grief.

Sandy and Diane also worried that they didn't know what was current. They'd hear people talking about a television comedy or a movie that the two of them had never seen. At first they still referred to various objects by their familiar African names: wearing "tackys" to "swot" (sneakers to school), passing a "kombi" on the "tarmac" (a Volkswagen van on the highway). But other kids gave them strange looks: What planet had they just stepped off? So they changed the way they talked. And they learned not to ask for explanations of things they weren't familiar with because of the reaction they got from other kids, who couldn't believe that anybody alive could be so out of touch. After a while, they had the impression that people were looking at them strangely. Could it be that they were eating with the wrong utensils or wearing peculiar clothes?

So what did our daughters do to overcome their sense of separateness from other American kids? Well, to begin with, they found acquaintances and companions among other MK's and overseas types like themselves. They found others who knew a few words of Swahili, who understood what they were talking about when they spoke of climbing Mount Kilimanjaro or spotting game in Amboseli—people who empathized with them.

But as their circle of acquaintances and companions grew into a core of friends, they met and grew close to people from Oshkosh and Mason City and Paducah—places nowhere nearly as exotic as Nairobi but with cultures and customs just as significant to their citizens. They discovered that people are people, that there's more to life than maintaining foreign habits and strange ways just for the sake of keeping one's identity as an expatriate. They came to realize that, while living overseas had been a rich experience, attempting to relive it on an American college campus was worse than futile—it was downright anti-social. What's more, they came to see that those college students who insisted on wearing their native dashiki or headdress weren't just trying to keep their ties with the past; they were attempting to appear odd for oddness' sake.

In short, our daughters came to see that they were no longer Americans in Kenya—now they were Americans in the United States. And a new situation meant adaptation.

WHAT CAN YOU AND YOUR PARENTS DO?

Whether you leave home and go to college from halfway around the world or from across the county line, you and your parents need to keep the lines of communication open between you.

The telephone lines, yes. Maybe a set time on Sunday afternoon, when the long-distance rates are cheaper, is a good time for a weekly chat. Spontaneous calls when you just need to hear a voice from home will also be a good pick-me-up for your spirits.

But don't just call. Take the time to write a note to your parents. It doesn't have to be anything fancy—just tear a page out of your looseleaf notebook and scribble a few words. Send a clipping from the college newspaper. Send a photo your roommate took of you at the football game. Send a souvenir from the college store. Give your parents a decal for the back window of the family car and turn them into school supporters.

Tell them how grateful you are for the opportunity they've given you to attend college. Tell them that you love them.

Parents can reciprocate by sending money. Sending food. Sending letters and photos and church bulletins and hometown newspapers and anything that says, "We love you and miss you, and we're proud of you."

CHAPTER 8

GPA: Preparing for Academics

When you're in college, it's fun to play football or join a sorority or do any number of other interesting things. But the primary reason for going to college is to continue your education—to continue gaining the knowledge that will equip you for a productive and responsible adult life.

This isn't news to you, of course. If you've qualified for admission to college, you've heard many a high school teacher, counselor, or other administrator tell you much the same thing. And maybe it's very important to your parents that you get good grades. Maybe they expect your GPA to be high, expect to see your name on the dean's list of academic honors.

Maybe you've attended a college-prep school— a private academy or a public high school in a community whose citizens pay high taxes to support a high quality of education for their kids. If so, you're certainly not unfamiliar with the challenge of demanding academic work, day after day in class, night after night in homework.

But maybe you've been attending a school that hasn't put that much emphasis on academic hard work. A school where you're laughed at if you're a scholar, where few of the teachers expect you to study at home—certainly never over the weekend. You may be one of the many high-school graduates who've managed to make it through most of their secondary school years without ever having to write an essay or read an entire novel or speak a foreign language or solve a math problem beyond long division or watch a test-tube bubble over or investigate a local political issue.

If that's been your experience, then you're in for a rather rude shock as a freshman. But even if your high school has been quite rigorous academically, you'll still be facing some changes. Let's talk about some of the differences you can expect.

DIFFERENT LANGUAGE

You've got to learn the language of college academic life right away. Otherwise, when you overhear one sophomore tell another something like this, you'll wonder if you've been beamed to another planet:

> "Yeah, I missed pre-registration, and that really messed up my major. So my ac/ad tried getting me into some slide, but Rocks for Jocks was closed, and by the time I got to drop/add, I had no choice but the social science distrib, so I signed up pass/fail 'cause I didn't have the right prerecks for my minor, even though I'm pretty sure I'll withdraw and try to get some credits through core courses . . ."

They're not using a foreign language—they're using the kinds of terms that we explain in our glossary in Chapter Eleven.

One place to begin learning the language is the college catalog. Your high school probably didn't have anything like this—a big, thick paperback volume with lots of tiny print. It pays to read that fine print. It spells out the details that will govern your life for the next four years.

Of course, nobody but a professor speaks in catalog language. What you'll hear—in the Student Union, in the cafeteria line—is the slang that students use. Don't worry about the language. You'll pick it up easily enough.

DIFFERENT PLANNING

In an earlier chapter we cautioned you about making sure you get the right high-school diploma. You need an academic diploma, not a general diploma, to certify you for college entrance. Arranging that is fairly simple: all you have to do is make sure that your school counselor places you on the college-bound track.

But college is different. You have a lot more to say about the courses you take as you map out the territory of knowledge you expect to explore.

Sometime early in the summer following your senior year, you'll receive—along with your housing and meal-plan information—an academic planning guide, perhaps including the name of a faculty member who's been assigned to be your freshman adviser. The planning guide will outline your college's approach to educating its students. Some colleges let you choose whatever courses you want right from the start. They let you declare and begin working toward a major—which means you get to concentrate on one specific field of study (European history or music theory or civil engineering)—early on, without spending much time at all on unrelated subjects. Other colleges insist that you begin with general education; they have required courses that every freshman must take, a core of overlapping subjects that's central to their curriculum. Still others regulate the courses you take in both your freshman and your sophomore years, requiring you to distribute your time among several different departments or divisions and to take a variety of courses from each before allowing you to begin the process of selecting your own concentrated course of study.

Most colleges assign numerical credits to each course— two, three, or four credits—depending on the number of hours per week the class meets. To graduate, you'll need to accumulate the required number of credits, usually something like 120 credits over four years. Typically, you'll take five courses worth three credits each per semester, which means that in a year you'll have thirty credits, and in four years you'll have the required 120 credits.

But it's not enough just to take courses adding up to 120 credits. You have to take the right courses, sometimes in a prescribed order, with the successful completion of one course a prequisite to admission to another course. In addition, some courses that may sound very interesting in the college catalog are closed to non-majors or are open only to juniors and seniors.

You'll spend a lot of time studying your college catalog, working out the various possibilities for each semester's course load. After your first semester, you'll also be able to plan ahead and take part in pre-registration, which is a period when students already enrolled get first crack at the course schedule they want, ahead of newcomers. Pre-registration happens well in advance of the beginning of the next semester.

DIFFERENT SCHEDULE

The next noticeable difference will be your class schedule. Instead of having a high-school administrator assign you to English class in first period and algebra class in second period, you'll actually determine much of your own daily schedule for each semester or term as it comes along.

Depending on the size of your college and its approach to general education, you'll have a more or less wide-open choice of class meeting-times and days of the week. That's certainly going to be a novelty. Let's use English 101, the writing course most freshmen are required to take, as an example. In most high schools, English is a daily class; in college it's offered in two packages: Monday–Wednesday–Friday for 50 minutes each session or Tuesday–Thursday for 75 minutes per session. In addition, at any large university, you might have as many as 40 or 50 or more different "sections" or class meetings to choose from. It's up to you to pick one of those sections, such as the M–W–F 8:00–8:50 morning class or the T–T 1:00–2:15 afternoon section, depending on what suits you and the rest of your schedule.

Making up your course schedule is like putting a puzzle together. Your academic adviser should work out a four-year plan with you, but such plans often change as your interests change. Or your adviser may be too rushed to take as much time as you need. So a lot of such decision-making will be left up to you, and you have a lot of freedom to make those choices, in spite of your college's requirements.

Each semester you'll start by deciding how many credits you plan to take, asking yourself questions like these:

Can I carry a normal load and still have time

- to work a part-time job?
- to participate in sports?
- to work on the college newspaper?
- to play in the marching band?
- to work in student government?
- to have a social life?
- to work on the campus chapel committee?

Can I carry a normal load, or do I have to take on an extra course because

- I failed a three-credit course last semester and have to catch up?
- I'm expecting to have to work more hours next year, so I'd better try to get ahead of schedule now?
- the professor I want is going away on leave next year?

- the course I want is only offered in alternate years?
- the course I want is the most popular on campus, and if I don't sign up now, I might get closed out?

Can I carry a normal load, or do I have to cut back a course or two because

- I failed a tough course and I need to put in more time to pass it the second time around?
- I expect to work more hours at my job next semester?
- the debate team travels a lot during the spring, and I hope to make the traveling squad?
- band rehearsals cut pretty deeply into my study time, but I don't want to give up playing in the band?

Once you know how many credits you intend to carry, you look for those courses you have to take to fulfill the college's core requirements or those still remaining as part of your distributive requirement or those your major department expects of you, as well as any electives that might interest you. Then it's time for you to play the cut-and-paste game of trying to put together the best daily schedule you can.

Do you start your day early? Most college students try to avoid early-morning classes because they like to sleep in. That means most early classes are smaller than their mid-morning counterparts. If you can stand the 6:30 a.m. alarm clock, try to get as many of your tough courses scheduled for the earlier hours, when you're at your best. Or head for the popular course whose later sections may fill up.

If, on the other hand, you're a night person who likes to sleep late, you might want to load up on those Tuesday-Thursday classes that are offered from mid-morning to late afternoon. And if you're accustomed to an afternoon nap, you'll want to avoid those classes scheduled from 2:00 to 4:00 p.m.—the doldrums period. There's no point in committing yourself to attend those classes if you know you're going to nod off every afternoon.

You'll want to factor in your eating habits too. Is it important to you to eat lunch at noon? If so, plan your classes so that you make it to the lunch line early enough to have time to digest your food before racing off to your one o'clock lab.

When does your employer expect you to work? When does your a capella choir rehearse? When does the swimming team practice? When does your church hold its midweek service for college students? These and many other considerations will shape your schedule each semester—and much of that shaping will be in your hands.

Let's suppose you settle on five courses—all of them required—for your first semester as a freshman. They turn out to be Mathematics 101: Introduction to Calculus, English Composition 101, third-semester French, the History of Western Civilization, and Foundations of Psychology. With these classes, your schedule might look something like this:

	MON	TUE	WED	THUR	FRI
8:00	English		English		English
9:00		Western Civ		Western Civ	
10:00	Calculus		Calculus		Calculus
11:00	French		French		French
12:00					
1:00		Psychology		Psychology	

This represents a fairly typical academic agenda, sometimes called "three and two," meaning that three days a week you have three classes, and the other two days you have just two classes. This is a big change from the daily sameness of your high-school schedule.

DIFFERENT FIELDS

During your freshman year (and possibly the first semester of your sophomore year), you'll be determining the field of study you most enjoy, the area of knowledge that most intrigues you. It may be accounting or archaeology, biology or biblical studies, chemistry or choreography. It may be the same interest that brought you to this particular college in the first place, or—and there's a good chance this will happen—it may turn out to be the farthest thing from your original intention.

Whatever that field of knowledge, it becomes your major focus of study and learning. Usually before the second semester of your sophomore year, your college will ask you to declare your major as a formality so that the department you've chosen can take you into its care and provide adequate instruction, counsel, and even career placement for you.

You'll have to make that decision based on your experience in high school (if you were pretty good in calculus, the math requirements for civil engineering won't faze you), your experience with introductory courses in a particular college department, and your developing (and changing) interests. Maybe you've struck up a pleasant acquaintance with a particular professor; maybe you've attended a lecture that opened your eyes to a subject you'd never thought about before; maybe your roommate has told you about the great courses she's taking in art history; maybe you discover that you understand poetry better than you thought you would. Maybe your parents have offered a wise suggestion.

All these influences and suggestions come together in a strong sense of comfort and well-being whenever you talk about the field of your major academic interest. You know that, for now, that's what you want to spend most of your time studying.

Don't worry if what interests you most doesn't necessarily connect with anyone else's ideas about why you went to college. Some people regard a college education as a preliminary to getting a job. Isn't that *why* you go to college—to prepare for a job? Yes and no. Yes, if by "yes" you mean that the education you receive ought to make you a better prospect for some worthwhile profession or occupation. But no, a college education isn't supposed to be specifically job training; it's *education*, illumination, expansion of your vision, the shaping of your view of the world, the tearing down of walls your childhood understanding of life may have erected. College is the time for experiment and enlightenment, not drill work in job skills.

Anyone who tells you otherwise doesn't understand the purpose of *education* as distinct from *training*. If it's training you want, go to a technical or vocational school. If what's most important to you is landing a job, the best place for you is probably an employment agency.

On the other hand, if it's *education* you're after—a broader understanding of the human race and our history, our arts and literature, our curiosity about the nature of plants and animals and stars, our desperate desire to know where we came from and where we're going, our insatiable hunger for Someone or Something to worship, our unquenchable thirst for answers to the question "Why?"—if it's your ambition to find your own answers, then you've made the right choice in deciding to go to college.

Don't be surprised if, halfway through your junior year, you suddenly discover a section of the college catalog you've never noticed before, or a suite of offices in a building you've never visited before. "Department of Anthropology" says the sign over the bulletin board, and as you read its notices, you feel a strange pull to learn more about what goes on in those offices and classrooms. Before you know it, you're in your adviser's office, explaining why you want to switch your major from computer science to anthropology.

This isn't unusual. Lots of students change their majors and not necessarily as a result of some whim or irresponsible impulse. Sometimes a summer job in a different environment—being a counselor at a camp for handicapped kids, perhaps, or working as a filing clerk in an attorney's office—changes your perspective on what you want to do with your life. Sometimes an academic setback alters things—makes it clear, for example, that inorganic chemistry and you are never going to get along, which makes medical school somewhat unattainable. Or maybe you've attended a lecture or a presentation by a foreign diplomat or missionary and now suddenly see how people in other parts of the world live and how you might make a difference in their lives.

Changing your major can be risky, but it can also be a sign of maturity to admit the fact that the field you chose originally just doesn't interest you anymore—or at least doesn't interest you as much as your new area of studies. Of course, if you wait until late in your academic career, there may be a price to pay for changing. You may have run out of time to make the switch inside the customary four-year span; you may have to increase your load to work in the fundamental courses your new major requires. Summer school and an additional semester or two may be necessary.

But isn't it more important to settle on the right major than to keep on studying what no longer appeals to you as much as it once did?

DIFFERENT RESPONSIBILITIES

Once you've chosen your freshman courses and arranged a schedule that suits you, it's almost entirely up to you whether or not you go to class. No more compulsory attendance laws. No more relying on your mom or dad to get you up in the morning. It's all up to you, to your common sense and your sense of responsibility.

Very few colleges have rigid policies on class attendance. You might meet the rare professor who announces that she intends to take attendance and will issue grades accordingly, but there aren't many of her kind left. More often your teachers leave attendance up to you—and leave passing the class up to you.

If you have an older brother or a friend whose college road has been a little rocky, and if you can get him to tell you why, most of the time he'll confess that his academic problems began when he started cutting classes—when he started sleeping in or watching TV or getting distracted by romance or maybe getting too tied up in some other worthwhile project, such as solving a computer problem in the physics department or helping finish up a dorm homecoming float. Nothing illegal or immoral, but one thing leads to another, and pretty soon cutting classes gets to be normal.

Or your friend discovers that she's falling behind in a particular class, and she can't face going to the lectures and not understanding the professor. So she avoids the embarrassment by not showing up at all. Then it's time for the midterm test, and she can't face that, either. Then suddenly it's finals—and she finds herself confronted with the prospect of failing the course.

These kinds of problems are understandable, but they're also preventable. If you learn to manage the time you have before, between, and after classes, and you exercise a little self-discipline, you should be able to stay on top of your studying.

Every freshman should ask this question:
Am I going to spend my free time effectively

- by going to the library to do reserve reading?
- by going to the library to study?
- by catching up on much-needed sleep?
- by working at my part-time job?
- by writing letters?
- by helping out in some volunteer service?
- by getting involved in student activities?

Or am I going to waste time and money

- by playing video games at the Student Union?
- by gabbing with my friends in our room or dorm lounge instead of getting my homework done?
- by playing cards all night?
- by shooting pool in a local bar?
- by cruising the neighborhood in my friend's car?
- by watching the "soaps" every afternoon?

How you use or misuse your time is entirely up to you.

DIFFERENT INSTRUCTION

Along with a different academic schedule, you'll probably encounter a different form of instruction in some of your courses—the lecture method, sometimes the lecture–discussion method. Of course, just like your high-school teachers, some of your college teachers will sit on the edge of the classroom desk and casually but effectively lead your class through a series of questions, exploring the day's topic and raising some issues not covered in your textbook. Others will rely on students' reactions to the reading or lab work being done.

But some of your professors will offer you an entire semester of carefully prepared, thought-provoking talks. A few of them may invite your comments during their remarks, but others will expect you not to interrupt them. Instead, you'll be expected to listen carefully and take notes, then offer comment and criticism or ask questions following the lecture.

In some colleges and universities, lecturing is the teaching method most frequently used, especially for huge classes. For instance, we know of at least one major university with a freshman chemistry course that's taught by lecture in two sections, with 1200 students in each section. Needless to say, asking questions in this context isn't an option. Instead, students wait until the third class meeting each week, which is a "section meeting" or a "tutorial," a group of 20 or 25 students led not by the professor—students see him only at the podium on his lecture days—but by a graduate student who's working as a graduate assistant or a graduate fellow. This person receives a small stipend to help pay for his own studies in exchange for leading this kind of section once a week. The graduate student isn't on his own; he meets with the professor and other section leaders on a regular basis. Graduate assistants usually give a common quiz; they grade the midterm and final exams for the professor; often they also read the term papers students write. Frankly, in the larger universities, a student is known by name only to his section leader. To the professor, he's just a face in the crowd.

He sits through Monday's and Wednesday's lectures, hoping to learn enough to pass the quiz on Friday, hoping he can still remember the question he wants to ask but has to wait to ask the graduate assistant in Friday's section meeting.

This sounds boring—and it might be. A bad lecture badly delivered—or even a good lecture badly delivered—can be a deadly experience. But lectures of whatever quality are an inescapable fact of college life. On the surface, it seems as though you're condemned to a system in which one person does all the talking while you and your classmates simply sit there.

How will you handle the lecture method? We suggest these strategies:

1. Treat each lecture as a dialogue between the lecturer and you.

It's hard to have a dialogue with only one person doing the talking, and in a sense that's what's happening. The professor talks, and you listen. But no real teacher, no effective lecturer, thinks of himself or herself as the only participant in the lecture method. Your professor expects you and your classmates to be responsive and thoughtful, not passive and vacant-minded. She shouldn't be the only one carrying on the dialogue.

Even as she speaks, you have to be actively engaged in listening, thinking, recording main points and defining key terms, anticipating, questioning, agreeing or disagreeing, clarifying ideas in your own mind, extending the professor's ideas, applying the points being made, connecting the minor issues with the major line of reasoning. In short, you need to be a part of the discourse, the conversation, going on between thinking people.

2. Learn to listen and concentrate on the lecture.

This won't be easy. You've grown up in a culture that communicates primarily by visual effects. TV commercials, full-page magazine spreads, billboards—all of these are intended to entertain as well as inform. Who besides the Sunday-morning congregation just sits and listens?

But now, for the sake of your own academic survival in college, for the sake of disciplining your mind to receive and retain verbal information delivered in a complex and lengthy speech, you have to master the art of listening and concentrating.

You can help yourself listen and concentrate if you

- attend class faithfully;
- prepare for the class and its lecture by doing the assigned homework;
- arrive as early as possible and get your notebook and textbook ready;
- decide when the professor steps to the podium to give the lecture your full attention; choose a seat in the lecture hall

as far away from distractions (e.g., a group of talkers) as possible;

• focus your eyes on the lecturer, not on the rest of the auditorium or the students around you;

• use any teaching device the professor offers (an outline, a slide presentation, a reference to textbook pages) to help you maintain your concentration;

• anticipate where the lecturer's line of reasoning is heading and try to reach the next point before he does.

3. Learn to record the essential content of the lecture with useful notes.

Some people listening to lectures go overboard, attempting to scribble down every word in personal shorthand. They end up with pages of scrawl nobody—including themselves—can read or understand. What's needed is the skill of seeing a lecture unfold like a journey, hearing the speaker's emphasis as she moves from point A to point B, following the progression of ideas from start to finish.

To do this, you need to know how to make and use an outline of a lecture's main points and subpoints. For instance, suppose you'd been listening to these last few pages instead of reading them. If you had been making a simple, workable outline of just the material under the heading "Different Instruction" (starting on page 132), it would look something like this:

I. *Kinds of instruction to expect in college*
   A. Small class lectures
   B. Large auditorium lectures
   C. Lectures 2 × per week; sections/tutorials
      1 × per week
      Usually no chance to ask questions; have to wait
      until end of lecture or even until section meeting

II. Strategies for survival
   A. Treat each lecture like dialogue between prof and me—*active engagement* important
   B. Listen & concentrate, which is helped by
      1. attending class regularly
      2. preparing—doing homework
      3. arriving on time, getting notebook/textbook ready
      4. focusing when prof starts speaking
      5. picking a seat where I won't be distracted
      6. looking at prof, not all around room
      7. taking advantage of whatever listening/ viewing help prof offers
      8. trying to figure out where prof's thinking is leading and getting there ahead of prof if possible
   C. Make useful notes
      1. outline properly
      2. write down only pertinent material

And that's where we are right now. By reviewing this outline, you can get a pretty good sense of what took us about five pages to express. Nothing beats a clear outline for helping you to organize and retain your information.

Once you've created an outline in class, you can use it to review and reinforce what you've learned. One good study technique is to try writing a summary of any major point in a lecture. So you might take the preceding outline and recreate any of its major points—or even one of its minor points—in a paragraph or two. When you can do that a week or ten days after the lecture, you know you've mastered the twin arts of listening to and retaining information.

But for some students, pen and paper are too old-fashioned, too much work. They prefer modern technology, so they bring along a tape recorder to the lecture hall. They sit back and relax, confident that the tape has all the vital information. Recording a lecture they hope will turn out to be significant makes sense; listening to it later on may even be inspiring. But when do they have time to play back all those 45-minute lectures? What's the point of spending twice the time—in class, then back at the dorm—listening to the same lecture? Why not take good notes the first time around, then review them?

DIFFERENT EXPECTATIONS

Besides expecting you to take good notes in class, your professors have a few other expectations.

1. You're expected to use the library.

Bill called home in mid-October of his freshman year, upset about his midterm grades. He'd been faithfully attending his classes; he'd read all the assigned chapters in his textbooks; he'd turned in his work on time. He thought he was ready to ace the midterms. Instead, he'd turned up C's and D's.

"It wasn't fair," he told his father on the phone. "I knew everything that was in the textbook and in my lecture notes. But they asked other stuff I'd never even heard of."

"Was there a reserve reading list?" Bill's father asked him.

"Huh?"

Unlike most high-school instruction, college instruction often isn't limited to what's in the textbook(s) or what's talked about in class. Frequently you're expected to do additional work in the library—like reading parts of, some of, or all of the books on what's called the reserve list.

Probably at the first meeting of each class, each professor will hand out a course calendar (also called a syllabus), showing the important dates throughout the semester. Really well-organized professors will have each class meeting listed, maybe even noting a lecture or discussion topic and the reading or lab work due by that date. The syllabus specifies the dates of major tests or exams and shows you when your major writing assignments or completed experiments are due.

But the syllabus will also include a reading list or bibliography for the course: maybe a half-dozen or maybe twenty different books. You aren't expected to go out and buy all those books; you may not even be expected to read more than a couple of chapters in any of them. But your professor in that particular class feels that, for you to get a balanced view of the subject, you need more than his lectures and more than the opinions of your textbook author. You need to supplement your learning with additional information gained by reading beyond the limits of his classroom.

So the professor requests that the library set aside these books, removing them from general circulation and placing them on a shelf of books reserved for students taking that particular course. That means these books will be available only on a restricted basis—perhaps for as few as two or three hours per stretch in the library (though they can be checked out more than once), or overnight (with a heavy penalty for late return). Occasionally they might be on two- or three-day reserve.

Books on reserve may not necessarily be set aside just for your section. Your professor and his colleagues may teach several sections of the same course, and all their students may need to read the same 40-page chapter on why dinosaurs became extinct—a challenge when there are only two copies of the book in your college library. Imagine the hassle a day or two before midterms—a good reason to get the reserve reading done ahead of schedule.

This brings up the matter of ethics in using a library and its resources. Any academic institution—from preschool to university—shares its books with all those who need and enjoy them. If anyone "borrows" a book and doesn't return it, that careless person deprives the next person of the chance to learn from that book. It's especially true if the library has only limited quantities of the book or the book is on reserve for many people's use. Also inconsiderate is the person who tears a page out of a book because he's too lazy to copy down a significant paragraph or too cheap to pay for photocopying. Colleges are very protective of their books, so they have ways of detecting such crimes. Even at most evangelical Christian colleges, you'll see an electronic device at the library door that picks up signals from any book or document or audio recording or videotape that hasn't been properly checked out. When that buzzer sounds, it means a thief has been caught, and penalties can be severe.

Don't make Bill's mistake and find yourself taken by surprise on the freshman midterms. Learn to find your way around your college library. Besides holding the greatest wealth of knowledge you've yet encountered, it's probably the best place to study on a regular basis. And there's a good chance you'll meet your kind of people in the library. That's where Don and Belinda met, at the end of their freshman year. Four years later, they met at the altar.

2. You're expected to make and keep office appointments during your professors' office hours.

Unlike your high-school teachers, every member of the college faculty has office space in or near the suite of offices that makes up the headquarters of his or her department. In high school, if you had a question or a problem to discuss with your teacher, you went to her classroom, unless she happened to be a department chairperson.

That's not the usual way to meet your college teachers. In general, you'll find that your professors prefer to meet you at an appointed time and place, customarily at their office. On each office door you'll find posted that professor's office hours, something like this: M–W 2:00–4:00; F 2:00–3:00.

Generally speaking, a professor likes to meet with his students—but it's also part of his contract with the college to make time available for such meetings. So take advantage of his being there. You might want to talk over a current issue or ask a question too involved for class or discuss some matter that's grown out of your reading for his class. Or you may need to inquire about your grade on the last essay. Or, if you've been absent because of illness or another legitimate reason, you may need to ask for help over the short term to get yourself back on track.

Maybe the professor will suggest that the two of you go over to the Student Union for a cup of coffee. If he or she is part of a very congenial faculty on a campus that prides itself on maintaining close relationships between faculty and students, you might be invited, along with others, to the professor's home for an evening.

But remember, you're only one of several dozen (or hundred) students, many of whom may need to spend some time with this same faculty member. So use your common sense and be sure to

- keep your appointment;
- arrive promptly;
- state your business;
- watch the time—don't stay beyond your allotted time.

A gentle word of caution: No matter how much you may admire your professor, keep that admiration at an academic level. In other words, don't get emotionally entangled with any of your teachers. Every professional educator—like every physician and attorney and pastor—knows that helping people sometimes leads to personal dependence. From such dependence springs affection, which can lead to romantic involvement. In turn, such involvement between students and faculty generally leads to chaos. And keep in mind that most colleges prefer not to have their professors dating students.

Different Grading

What's the top grade in your high school? 100% or A+ or 4.0? And how frequently do you reach that peak?

Whatever your grading system, remember that all grades are merely symbolic. They represent a form of comparison. Grades attempt to show how you stack up when your work is compared with that of others. The greater the number of participants being ranked, the greater the possibility of achieving a valid comparison. When you write a fairly decent essay that turns out to be the best among the two dozen in your class, your teacher may give you a grade of A or even A+. But how do you know it's really that good? Suppose you submitted that same essay to a city-wide or state-wide competition of some sort. Would it still rank at the top? How would it rate in a national test, such as the College Board's English Composition Achievement Test? In other words, realistically speaking, what's your level of ability?

When it comes to grades, many college professors seem to feel obliged to give freshmen a helpful dose of reality. It's often been said that there's nothing like the first batch of freshman grades to humble the proud. You may have been a member of the Cum Laude Society, you may have been elected to the National Honor Society, but none of that means anything to the professor of your introductory psychology class. He's measuring your performance by a different set of standards.

So be prepared for a somewhat different set of grades from those you've known and been proud of. Not just a different system but a different outcome—your grades will probably fall into a decidedly lower range. But you'll work yourself back up the scale soon enough.

What's really different is how those grades are determined. Except at places like West Point and Annapolis, where daily quizzing still goes on in some courses, you'll almost never face the kind of step-by-step evaluation you've become familiar with in high school. Every professor, every department, and every college sets its own policy on grades, so in any given semester you could have five different standards of measurement, one for each course. The following scenario will illustrate the point.

Your English instructor announces that you'll write a 500-word composition every week for twelve weeks, then take three weeks to write a major paper. Those thirteen assignments will produce your grade. No final exam during December's semester exam period.

Your math professor promises a weekly quiz, a midterm, and a two-hour final.

Your French teacher informs you that there will be frequent vocabulary quizzes, tests of your ability to read, speak, and understand the language, a midterm exam, and a final that will include an oral test.

Your Western Civ professor wants four "brief" papers, 1000-1500 words each, on various historical and cultural developments. No quizzes, no midterm, no final.

Your psychology teacher requires you to present a "research paper," assuming that you know what that's going to entail. He doesn't give you any definition of what he wants or any indication of its length or scope. He simply warns that if it's not satisfactory, he'll offer you a chair in the final exam room.

Five different courses, five different sets of expectations, five different standards to meet, five different point systems to be assessed by. And five different timetables to follow:

Daily (3 × each week)	French and possibly math
Weekly	English and math
Periodically (4 ×)	Western Civ
Midterms	French and math
Long-term	Psychology
End-of-term	English, math, French; threat of psychology

You can see why the college bookstore sells those oversized deskpad calendars.

With so many different types of assignments throughout the semester, the value of time management—the effective planning and use of your time—becomes paramount. You simply can't survive in college academics without knowing how to keep every spare minute from being wasted. Of course you need to make time for recreation and a social life. But how to get your work done and save some time for those other activities that keep you well-balanced will be a constant challenge. To be a college student is to be pressed for time. It goes without saying.

DIFFERENT CONSEQUENCES

And what if you don't meet the deadline? What if your work falls below the level of acceptability? What if you get terrible grades the first semester?

Don came home following that first wonderful semester at Chapel Hill to enjoy Christmas with his family. He was having a great time. New friends, new freedom, the prospects of a successful indoor track season just ahead. And now a happy reunion for the holidays.

There was just one cloud on the horizon: grades were due in the mail any time after New Year's Day.

Throughout the holidays Don kept one eye on the mailbox. He wasn't looking for Christmas cards. On the morning he was returning to college, Don and his father were just backing out of the driveway, en route to the airport, when the US Postal Service Jeep came down the road. Don's father stopped the car and reached through the window for the bundle of post-Christmas bills and flyers. In the middle of the batch lay a computer-printed envelope addressed to Don. Knowing the law about the rights of college students, Don's father passed the envelope over to his son and drove toward the airport.

Don winced as he opened the envelope, then passed it back to his father.

"I'm sorry, Dad," he said.

The news was abysmal. Although Don had been a cum laude graduate of a fine school just six months before, his grades had fallen to a level threatening his right to stay in college, never mind his eligibility to compete in track. Although his father was instantly angry, he didn't react outwardly. Instead, he slowed the car to say, "Do we need to talk with your coach about this?"

"No, sir."

"Then only you can do something about it."

And Don did. In addition, when he later returned to the University of North Carolina as head coach of track and field, he instituted a policy for his freshman athletes. He required them to spend four evenings a week in the university library, Monday through Thursday, from 7:30 to 9:30, for three consecutive weeks. A team manager checked them in and checked them out. Those who had perfect attendance were released; others remained in the compulsory study program until they had achieved perfect attendance. In this way Don encouraged them to develop regular library-study habits.

The point is this. In high school a student can sink almost all the way to the bottom before anybody gets after him. After all, compulsory attendance laws in every state seek to keep students *in* school, not throw them out.

College is different. Most colleges have minimum standards that a student must meet to remain "in good standing." A freshman will not be advanced to sophomore standing without achieving a certain GPA; a sophomore will not be advanced to junior standing unless he or she meets an even higher standard. Admission to undergraduate majors or pre-professional programs such as pharmacy, journalism, nursing, pre-med, pre-dental, and pre-law is dependent on achieving an acceptable GPA.

Then there's your eligibility for athletics or student government or other co-curricular activities. The NCAA demands a

2.0 academic average each semester. Each college sets its own criteria for those who want to run for student office or edit the newspaper or hold other leadership positions.

So there are serious consequences to slacking off academically. A student could lose everything in a single semester. But there are also wonderful consequences awaiting the student who works hard and succeeds. Graduate scholarships and fellowships for foreign study, commissioning as an officer in the military branch of his choice, invitations to join thriving companies as a junior executive: eventually the prospect of making one's own choice of a career or a calling to serve others, rather than settling for something else.

These opportunities can be yours if you're willing to work for them.

CHAPTER 9

Roaring Lions: Challenging What You've Been Taught to Believe

The authors of this book first met in Africa. One of our early adventures together as two families was visiting the great game parks in Kenya. There we saw and learned to respect the king and queen of the beasts, the lions who rule. We learned to listen in the night for the unmistakable sound of a lion's roar—a deep, coughing sound signaling to every other animal within earshot that a kill has been completed and a meal is about to begin. In the morning we'd find the remains of a zebra or gazelle, clear evidence of the lion's fearsome power.

Once, on an overnight visit to the game reserve at Amboseli, we were strictly warned by park officials not to leave our cabins during the night. When we inquired why, they told us in graphic and sickening detail about a young American tourist who just the week before had ignored those same warnings and been torn to pieces just outside her cabin door.

Those docile lions you see in television commercials for investment companies and copier manufacturers are probably drugged; they aren't anything like the real thing. If you go to the Rift Valley in East Africa, be prepared to meet up with lions that are anything but tame.

And when you go to college, be prepared to meet a few untamed lions there too. They won't be as easy to detect as you might wish. Their looks might fool you, and they won't necessarily go around making frightening noises. But if you pay careful attention, you'll be able to heed the warning issued by the Apostle Peter:

> Be self-controlled and alert. Your enemy the devil prowls around like a roaring lion looking for someone to devour. (1 Peter 5:8)

AVOIDING THE LIONS' DEN

Going to college is a wonderful opportunity for you to grow strong in mind and spirit. Overall, going to college can be, should be, and probably will be a happy experience. But it's not without a potential for danger, which can take many forms:

- *dangerous experiments*
- *dangerous habits*
- *dangerous rejection of cause and effect*
- *dangerous relationships*

Notice that we didn't say anything about "dangerous ideas" or "dangerous books." Some people fear ideas at least as much as nuclear bombs, and no wonder: ideas have tremendous power to shake and disrupt and make us uncomfortable. Think what it must have been like when someone first suggested the idea that this planet may not be the center of the universe. We know what happened to Galileo. Remember how shocked most people were when the idea arose that women might vote, that blacks might run for office, that a Roman Catholic might be elected president of the United States?

The same can be said about books. Through the centuries, various books have shaped the thinking of political leaders and social reformers. When President Abraham Lincoln met Harriet Beecher Stowe, the author of *Uncle Tom's Cabin,* he said to her, "So, you're the woman who wrote the little book that started the big war!"

But are books and the ideas they contain "dangerous" in themselves? Some people think so. At the commencement exercises of a Baptist college, the elderly chairman of the trustees was assisting the president in handing out diplomas. Suddenly, during a lull in the procession of graduates across the stage, the old man grabbed the microphone and in woeful earnestness said, "I want all you parents out there to know that your sons and daughters have had a safe education."

Obviously, here was a man who, despite his position at the head of a college's governing board, feared that dangerous ideas might have been infiltrating the minds of students. What made him feel secure was his certainty that it hadn't happened at his college. If he was right, you can imagine what kind of education those graduates received.

A college education isn't worth very much if all you get out of it is a reinforcing of what you already know and believe. That's not education—that's indoctrination, the kind of training we give to dogs in obedience school to insure the same learned response every time we issue a command. A good college education ought to broaden your mind with fresh ideas and fresh concepts that challenge your former assumptions and thereby either change what you believe or make your beliefs stronger.

The fact is that a belief system that's never been challenged is like a building or a bridge that's never felt the force of strong winds. How do you know it will stand when the hurricane strikes?

But while we can shake our heads at an old man's anti-intellectual fears, admitting the fact that dangers lurk on every college campus may be just as unpopular. Avoiding those dangers will call for strength of character that stands out in a crowd, that chooses to resist the strongest peer pressure of all—the insistence that "Everybody else is doing it."

MAKING YOUR OWN WISE CHOICES

Remember how it used to be? Mom used to make all the choices for you. From the time you were an infant until you were a toddler, she dressed you. As you grew older and more coordinated, you learned to dress yourself, but she still decided what you'd wear. The night before you started school, your mother laid out the clothes you'd wear the next day. When you were this age, she'd come home from a shopping trip with some new clothes for you: a skirt or pair of pants, a blouse or shirt, a pair of socks, some underwear. You had no say in her choice of colors or style. You didn't even know your own sizes.

But little by little, things began to change. Dad took you to the shoe store, where you were expected to pick out from the window display the shoes you'd like to try on. Then, with your first earnings from an after-school or summer job, you asked to go to the mall to look for a pair of jeans. Finally you reached the point of buying most of your own clothes, or at least picking out what you would and wouldn't wear.

Life is like that—a process of arriving at new stages of responsibility based on decision-making. We measure maturity not just by how old a person is but by the quality of choices he or she makes. Have you ever heard one adult tell another to stop being childish? It shows that it's possible to reach chronological adulthood without reaching emotional adulthood. It's an accusation of immaturity based on someone's acting like a spoiled child instead of like a responsible adult. And a responsible adult is what your parents hope you'll become.

DANGEROUS EXPERIMENTS

Carol was a freshman at Barnard College in New York City. She'd won a huge scholarship to study there in preparation for law school. Her parents were very proud of her, and while they might have preferred to have her attend college closer to home in Ohio, they knew she was very responsible.

During her first weekend at college, Carol met some young women who invited her to a party in the Morningside Heights district, near the campuses of Barnard and Columbia University. Carol found herself in an unfamiliar setting, with a smorgasbord of pills and powders, including cocaine. None of her close friends in high school had been casual cocaine users, but this group seemed to be in control of themselves. She felt awkward about admitting to them that she'd never snorted a line of cocaine before. Against her better judgment, she decided that just this once, while she was getting acquainted, to celebrate her arrival in New York . . .

She never recovered from the coma she fell into. She died in St. Luke's Hospital a few days later.

She was a victim of the roaring lion of peer pressure.

DANGEROUS HABITS

But, as we all know, many freshmen indulge in drugs without any high drama or life-threatening emergency. Many more spend most Saturday nights getting drunk. Apart from an occasional rotten hangover, nothing happens. So what's the big deal?

We want you to live free from slavery.

Have you ever watched a chain-smoker's fingers tremble

as he lights a fresh cigarette from the still-burning end of the one he's half-smoked? Ask him if he's a free man.

Have you ever watched an alcohol-dependent woman study the hands of the clock as they inch toward the hour when she'll permit herself the first drink of the day? Ask her if she's a free woman.

Have you ever seen a drug addict go cold turkey? Seen her clutch her body as she's wracked first by chills, then by fever?

Every one of those people started out free and ended up enslaved by a habit.

But there are other dangerous habits besides these which we also call substance abuse. How about some as common as these?

- *procrastination that leads to cheating*
- *borrowing without asking that leads to stealing*
- *sexual relations, whether with one person or more than one person, that lead to using other people*

These too are habit-forming behaviors whose hold becomes increasing difficult to break.

Start by putting off your major assignments until the night before they're due, and you'll find yourself deluded into thinking that you can always pull an all-nighter and get the paper in on time. Until the time when everything falls apart and you need the paper to insure a passing grade, so when someone down the hall offers you his paper from last term—or suggests that you buy a paper from a "black market" dealer—you take the dishonest way out. Your simple bad habit of procrastination may lead to cheating and plagiarism.

Start by asking to borrow a roommate's clothes or money. Then comes the time that he isn't there to ask, so you just take a jacket or a sweater or a ten-dollar bill because you're so sure he'd let you have it anyway. How quickly it becomes easy to help yourself to anyone's property.

Start by taking advantage of the absence of the roommate

of your new boyfriend or girlfriend and spend just one night of sexual intimacy. After that experience you'll find it hard to go back to the innocence of a good-night kiss at the dorm door. Yet you'll find yourself wondering *why* and *who else*, and when the almost inevitable day arrives that the two of you break up, you'll wonder *why* all over again. Remember, too, that reputations are fragile things, and this kind of behavior can make your reputation vulnerable to attack.

The roaring lion of habitual behavior strikes again.

DANGEROUS REJECTION OF CAUSE AND EFFECT

The real problem in all these examples is this: Most young people reject the law of cause and effect. They pretend that there's no connection between one event and another, no link between one action and a subsequent reaction, no consequences to human behavior.

In a scientific age, such an attitude is peculiar. With all the lab experiments to study chain reactions and other forms of step-by-step analysis, you'd think somehow the basic message would get through. *Fire burns.* If you hold your palm over a candle flame, the tissue of your skin will become scorched and painful. *Water drowns.* If you fall into the deep end of a swimming pool and can't swim to safety, your lungs will fill with water and you'll lose your life.

But while most people will concede to this simplified law of cause and effect, they don't want to carry the rule into moral areas of decision-making. It's easier and certainly more popular to act as if there's no connection between one thing and another. And, despite evidence to the contrary, the motto of most young people seems to be "It can't happen to me."

Remember those awful movies you had to watch in

driver's ed classes—the ones with the grotesque wrecks and the decapitated bodies flung all over the highway? But how many teenage viewers say to themselves, "If I drive recklessly, that could happen to me"? Not many, we guess.

This kind of thinking explains the rationalizations all of us have heard. Other people may become addicted to tobacco, but not me. Other people may develop tobacco-related tumors or breathing difficulties, but not me. Besides, smoking makes me look so sophisticated.

Other people may suffer from alcoholism, but not me. I can hold my booze; I can drink anybody under the table.

Other people may be too weak to pick and choose when they want to get high, but not me. I can start and stop using drugs whenever I want.

Other people may be bothered about compromising somebody else's personal integrity and invading their sexual privacy, but not me. I'm just satisfying natural drives. Other people may get a sexually transmitted disease, maybe even AIDS, but not me.

It won't happen to me because I'm invincible, immortal; I'm not subject to the natural law of cause and effect.

Maybe you know someone who thinks like that. Or maybe you know someone who takes the other side of denying cause and effect, which seems to be summed up by the crude phrases we see more and more often on bumper stickers and T-shirts. We've observed that people who wear these slogans on their caps or sweatshirts are often the sort who crave attention and like the fact that their bold vulgarity makes other people notice them. That's sad.

On the surface, such phrases seem to mean that, no matter what we do, nastiness or unpleasantness occurs. In a sense, of course, such statements are true, because any number of bad things happen that we have no control over. But such phrases also have about them a casual disregard for cause and effect. By their very outrageousness as stated philosophies of life, these slogans declare that the people who live by them aren't responsible for the condition of their lives.

Score another victory for the roaring lions.

DANGEROUS RELATIONSHIPS

Perhaps you've noticed that, over the past couple of years, your parents have begun to back off on making decisions about you and your friends. It's not that they're no longer interested in what you do or where you go and with whom. It's just that they're preparing you for the time when you and no one else will be deciding what's best for you in every area of your life: what your life's work will be; where you'll live; whether or not to marry and, if so, who that person will be; and—the most serious decision—what your relationship to God and others will be.

These are some of life's biggest decisions; no one else can make them for you. So if your parents are themselves wise decision-makers, they've already decided that it's time, in effect, to begin working themselves out of a job, the job of choosing which relationships are best for you.

You've already agreed with your parents on the choice to go to college; you've even decided *how* you're going to choose a college. But once that's behind you, wave upon wave of new decisions and new choices to make will roll in on you. Whether you ride the crest of each wave (and how well you do it) or get thrown into its shallows will depend on how wisely you choose each time you face a decision.

Wherever you choose to enroll—at a vast secular university, at a medium-sized, church-related college, or at a small evangelical Christian college—you'll soon realize that you're coming under the influence of some people who have an outlook on life that's entirely different from anything you've been taught to believe. And that's just as it should be.

After all, that's why you go to college in the first place: to learn from others. You could save a lot of money just by going to your local library each day, finding a quiet corner, and reading the classics. But, as Ralph Waldo Emerson noted over 150 years ago, there's something more to be learned than can be found in books. "Meek young men grow up in libraries," he said, "believing it their duty to accept the views which Cicero, which Locke, which Bacon, have given; forgetful that Cicero, Locke, and Bacon were only young men in libraries when they wrote these books." Ironic, isn't it? And it makes the point that your college education depends on something more than just what you read and study. To a great extent, it depends on whom you meet and admire and choose to emulate. It depends on what you hear other people say and then debate before you accept or reject their opinion. It depends on how well you develop your critical powers of judgment in choosing acquaintances and friends, some of whom become your real teachers.

Ellyn and her brothers all remember that many of their freshman classmates seemed preoccupied with getting drunk during the first few weekends in Chapel Hill. Many of these young people were from homes and communities where drinking alcohol was forbidden. (Drinking is a religious and cultural taboo in most Southern Baptist churches.) For the first time, they were free from parental guidance and scrutiny. They felt compelled to cut loose and get drunk whenever possible simply because they'd lived under such tight restrictions.

You're going to meet people like this—people from an environment even more sheltered than yours, people whose first year at college is their first time away from home. For them, college represents their first opportunity to assert their own personhood. You'll also meet people at the other end of the spectrum, people who are very cosmopolitan and sophisticated, who might feel that the university restricts rather than frees them. In fact, you'll meet people all along this spectrum. You'll meet people with no sense of purpose to their lives, and people who have every step of their future already surveyed and planned. People who live very healthy lives, and people whose nights and days are blurred by drugs and alcohol. People who can't say no to food, and people who are perpetually on the latest diet. People who never attend class and still make 4.0, and people whose study habits are obsessive. People who despise America's government and economy, and people who revel in the American political system and intend to make a career of it. People whose only religion is perpetual self-indulgence, and people earnestly committed to the teachings of some strange sect you've never heard of.

- *Will you be able to tell the genuine people from the phonies?*
- *Will you be able to tell the difference between people who have your best interests in mind and people who want to use you for their own interests?*
- *Will you be able to spot people whose attention-getting devices include outrageous, foolish, and even self-destructive behavior?*
- *Will you know the difference between "friend" and "acquaintance"?*

Just as you'll meet all different kinds of students, you'll meet professors whose ideas range all across the spectrum. You won't believe all or necessarily any of what you hear from some of these sources. The reason you'll accept one person's influence and resist another's won't simply be that one is more likable or more powerful than the other. The reason will be that you'll discover that you have something in common with this person which makes his or her new ideas appealing.

RECOGNIZING A DIFFERENT WORLDVIEW

What you'll be looking for is what we've earlier called a different outlook on life. Let's consider that figure of speech for a moment. It's part of a metaphorical description that at one time only philosophers seemed to understand; now you can find the term not only on a newspaper's editorial pages but also in the sports section. The term is "world-and-life view," sometimes shortened to "worldview." It's a way of saying that everyone—consciously or unconsciously—takes a position and adopts an attitude toward life. You might call it a point of view about the nature of life and what's important in life.

Several metaphors for life have entered our language as clichés: "the journey of life" and "the voyage of life"; life as a "rat race"; "the game of life." Then there's the popular bumper sticker reminding us that "Life's a beach." All these phrases describe worldviews—but what exactly do they mean?

If life is a journey, is it an up-and-down experience on a bumpy road, a smooth glide along a quiet country road, or the frustration of a jammed freeway at rush hour? If life is a voyage, is it a holiday cruise in tranquil tropical waters, or a stormy crossing on a small ship with a mad captain at the helm? If life is a clinical experiment, are you the observer overseeing the rats' maze, or are you in the box with the rest of the rodents? If life is only a game, an athletic contest, are you one of the star players or just a benchwarmer? Is your team winning or losing? And what does it really mean when someone says that "life's a beach"?

Early in *Hamlet*, Prince Hamlet describes life as "an unweeded garden / That grows to seed; things rank and gross in nature / Possess it merely." Imagine the royal palace and its carefully sculptured gardens. Now imagine those same palace grounds abandoned and overrun by foul-smelling weeds. That's Hamlet's worldview. But at this point, Hamlet has no inclination to do anything about the situation he describes. He isn't about to try to change anything in Denmark; he's merely an observer of the rotten conditions.

That's the way many people are. But recognizing and holding to a worldview ought to help you determine your values, your priorities, not leave you apathetic. If life is like a hospital's emergency room, are you an accident victim? Are you one of those committed to caring for the injured? Or are you merely an observer reporting life's tragedies? Are you passive, active, or neutral?

Throughout your college career, you're going to encounter a wide range of worldviews, from the familiar and conventional to the shocking and revolutionary. Some of these attitudes will be new to you; others will seem stale. Some of the most shocking may also turn out to be the most childish; on the other hand, what shocks you initially may also become a permanent part of your own worldview.

Following is a sample of the range of thought you'll find on many campuses. This isn't a complete chart of every possible worldview; it's just an attempt to depict the span of ideas you'll encounter. You'll find extremes on every line.

Regarding the meaning and purpose of life, you'll find professors and students alike who are, morally speaking,

careless / hedonistic / fun-loving / circumspect / overly cautious.

As far as politics are concerned, you'll meet those who represent viewpoints described as

anarchist / socialist / liberal / conservative / patriotic / apolitical.

When it comes to the existence of God, you'll find professors and students who are

disbelieving / unbelieving / doubting / questioning / believing.

(An unbeliever is one who simply professes not to believe in God, maybe because he's unsure or skeptical. A disbeliever not only rejects belief but also wants to discourage other people from believing; he's militantly opposed to belief in God.)

Even among those who call themselves Christians, you'll meet some people who seem to you to be

heretical / orthodox / evangelical / charismatic / fundamentalist / cultic.

On the other hand, from their point of view you may seem to be

bizarre / a little strange / conventional / old-fashioned.

On matters like abortion, you'll find people who hold to these differing positions:

total freedom of choice / limited freedom of choice / total abolition of choice.

On issues such as the legalization of currently banned drugs, you'll find people committed to

decriminalizing drugs / making drugs available to addicts only / passing tougher laws on drugs.

There's nothing dangerous in facing these tough issues and asking the right questions about them. In fact, it's this kind of diversity of opinion that makes a college community open to a multitude of answers to the major questions every thoughtful person asks:

- *What is life for?*
- *Why am I here?*
- *Where did I come from?*
- *Where am I going?*
- *How can I get the most out of my life?*

"AND GLADLY TEACH"

Both of us are teachers. We've taught in schools, colleges, and universities. We respect most of our colleagues in the profession for their commitment to knowledge and its significance in shaping our civilization. We can guarantee that, over the next four years or so, you'll meet some of the most dedicated, earnest, sincere, and caring people you'll ever know—they'll remind you of some of your best high-school teachers. These people will attract you because they're willing to give their time and eager to share their knowledge, and many of them will inspire you to make some contribution of your own to benefit the world. These will be professors who model their careers after the Oxford clerk of *Canterbury Tales*, about whom Chaucer wrote, "And gladly would he learn, and gladly teach."

Joyous learning leads to joyous teaching. You'll be impressed by women and men who know so much yet have the humility to recognize how much remains to be learned. From their example you'll learn to ask questions, to root out your own ignorance, and to dispel the darkness of your own prejudices.

Sometimes these teachers may scare you by leading you into areas of disputed opinion and speculation, where the outcome is uncertain. When this happens, you may think that the only safe response is closed-mindedness, but that's the very opposite of the reason for going to college.

A favorite phrase in education is "the quest for knowledge." It suggests a journey in search of truth, sometimes along a path whose next turn—never mind its final destination—may be unknown. You see, we don't study merely to confirm what we already know or to prove what we believe in advance to be true. That's called playing with loaded dice, which Albert Einstein said even God chooses not to do.

A lab researcher performing the same experiment for the

seventy-ninth time may be anticipating *verification* of every earlier experiment; but she's also prepared to expect that *this* time something new might occur. Yet many high-school graduates arrive at college unaware that their notions of reality and absolute certainty are about to be exploded by questions such as "How do you know?" "What makes you sure?" and "What evidence can you offer to prove what you claim is true?"

Your best teachers—and probably your favorite professors—will be those who challenge you with just such questions. But these teachers won't abandon you after challenging you; they'll help you search for the very answers you lack. This search becomes the most important part of your education because, in fact, it's the search for truth.

WHAT IS TRUTH?

The Latin word for truth is *veritas*. It serves as the motto or part of the motto for many colleges and universities, Harvard and Yale among them. Yet truth seems to be like quicksilver—impossible to grasp, beyond our power to bottle and contain, utterly elusive. Unless you happen to believe in a God whose principal attribute is truth and who reveals that truth with a wisdom that exceeds the capacity of human understanding. *Revealed truth* is the central message of the Bible: God reveals his Word to patriarchs and prophets, God reveals his Word in the person and gospel of Jesus of Nazareth, God reveals his Word through the Holy Spirit to the apostles and the church.

The Bible doesn't profess to tell all the truth there is to know. There's nothing in the Bible about test-tube babies or how to solve a geometry problem. But the Bible reveals truth about who we are and how we ought to live our lives, now and in the future.

For some people, that's too vague and intangible. The only

truth they want is *empirical,* truth that holds up under a kind of scientific testing. "Seeing is believing," they say, and truth exists only in the hard facts that have been repeatedly observed, recorded, and checked, proven by evidence. This is what's called the scientific method, and it's the approach to truth most often taken in the physical sciences, the natural sciences, and the social sciences.

Other people would say that truth is *interpretive* because data and facts tell only what happened, not the implications of what happened. Truth is more than what happened; truth is why it happened and with what results.

For instance, in 1927 Babe Ruth hit 60 home runs in 154 games. In 1961 Roger Maris hit 61 homers in 162 games. *Fact:* Maris hit more home runs than Ruth in a single major-league season. But can it then be said that Maris was a better slugger than the Babe? Or do the statistics need to be interpreted to learn the truth?

Still other people will tell you that truth is *experiential* and *emotional.* According to this view of truth, the way an individual acts and feels determines what's true and what isn't. This is commonly called a subjective attitude toward truth, and it governs most people's ethical and moral decisions. The standard defense of this attitude toward truth rests upon a single kind of assertion: "Well, the way I feel . . ." or "I think . . ." The big question is no longer "What is Truth?" The big question becomes "Is it true for me?"

So we find college couples living together, unashamed by what used to be considered by society (and still is, by law) an immoral relationship. But this doesn't matter to them. They've decided that living together without the bond of marriage is right for them, since marriage itself is just an old-fashioned notion, no longer "true" for them. In this decision they disregard both what the Bible teaches about fornication and what the law states. (Such a couple is in for a big surprise if they ever need to sign for each other's admission to a hospital, or vouch for each other's loan application at a bank, or try to re-enter the country as a couple, because they have no legal status as a couple.) By disallowing an absolute truth that is beyond their power to erase or re-write, the live-in pair, while claiming to be mature, is actually denying each other the single most mature decision they'll ever make: the decision to commit themselves to each other in a lifelong marriage.

Those who have a subjective attitude toward truth would argue that simply because you happen to believe that a particular act is wrong doesn't make it wrong for somebody else. Only if your view of what's true *for you* satisfies someone else's view of what's true *for him* can it be considered truth. Or so they say. This can be as confusing as it sounds.

Finally, some people hold that truth is purely *personal,* a private matter that's nobody else's business; truth is too intimate even to discuss. This attitude, called solipsism, rejects any authority outside oneself. It usually satisfies one's own prejudices about who's in control of the cosmos. It's also frequently scornful of any other approach to truth, especially if that approach happens to mention God.

THE MOST DANGEROUS PEOPLE YOU'LL MEET

We're sure you can handle most situations and the people involved in them. But we do want to warn you about some of the most dangerous people you'll meet in college or anywhere else.

The most dangerous people you'll meet are those who try to steal your mind, freeze your imagination, and paralyze your capacity to think and reason for yourself.

Some of the professors you meet may belong to that first group of people. Their attitude toward truth will express itself in an absurd claim: that no one can know the truth about anything. If anyone dares to suggest otherwise, these scholars will scornfully accuse him or her of being doltish, blind, brainwashed, uncritical (considered to be a particularly withering criticism), conventional, biased.

If you really want to see this kind of person in a frenzy, try suggesting that you believe truth can be known and—worse than that—you know truth because you know God. Then ask politely, "Professor, what authority do you recognize and submit to?" The basic issue that prevents him or her from acknowledging the reality of truth is this issue of *authority*. If truth exists, then some authority higher than us knows that truth, and that makes us subject to that authority. By denying the existence of truth, we can also withhold our submission to that authority.

There's a second, even more dangerous type who makes the opposite absurd claim: "I know the truth, and I'm the only one who can convey it to you." This is the assertion of the gurus who've decided that they possess a monopoly on truth, that they hold the only key to its secrets. These are what followers of Eastern mystical religions call "Perfect Masters."

This notion of all-knowing human beings is a powerful one. There are students in American colleges who chant the name of their Perfect Master before a midterm exam. There are corporate executives who pin a photograph of their Perfect Master to the back of the airplane seat ahead of them and focus on that photo in hopes of keeping the plane aloft. And on the fringes of evangelical Christianity—sometimes in the student body or even on the faculty of a Christian college—there are men and women who've developed a hypnotic spiritual power over gullible young people.

When you meet a ravenous lion, silence its roars just by knowing this fact and thanking God for it:

The greatest evidence that we've been created in the image of God is the fact that we, like God, possess the divine attributes of will, reason, and speech. No one can rob us of those gifts.

CHAPTER 10

Grace to Help
in Time of Need

Throughout this book we've tried to present a clear and fair picture of what going to college entails. We've touched on the positive points of the experience, because we believe your college years are bound to be exciting: You're a young and enthusiastic person in a community of other young and enthusiastic people, all of whom are reaching out for the future and its prospects. There's great potential there.

But we've also stressed some of the negative points of the experience, because we want to make sure you don't have unrealistic expectations. We've talked about many of these challenges, but we haven't said all we want to say about how to handle those difficult moments—better yet, how to avoid the worst of them.

If you profess to be a Christian—someone who has committed his or her life to Jesus Christ—then this chapter is directed especially to you. Whether you enroll at a huge state university or a small Christian college, you'll need to look for and find grace to help you in times of need.

GOD'S PROMISE TO YOU

The Bible promises us grace when we need it. In Hebrews 4:14-16, the writer describes our ascended Lord Jesus Christ as our "great high priest." He is holy and exalted, but he also is able to "sympathize with our weaknesses." Why? Because of the Incarnation, the experience of God-with-us that we celebrate every Christmas.

Born into this world, living as a human being, Jesus of Nazareth experienced what it's like to be lonely and unloved, hungry and thirsty, weary and discouraged, sorrowing and comforted, happy and overjoyed. What's even more striking is that Jesus of Nazareth was tempted to sin, and he could have yielded to those temptations. He was tempted to be a showman, tempted to challenge God the Father's authority, tempted to acknowledge Satan and join up with evil against holiness. He was tempted to follow popular opinion and get swept away by the crowd's cheers, tempted to ignore his Father's plan and establish his own agenda. He was tempted in every way, just as we are—yet was without sin. The fact that he didn't yield to sin makes Jesus Christ the only one eligible to redeem us from our sin.

Still, he "sympathizes with our weaknesses." Jesus Christ doesn't condemn us for feeling homesick or being envious of somebody else's better grades or lusting for some sexual thrill; he doesn't punish us for overeating or getting so down on ourselves that we want to go on a binge; he doesn't reject us because we're too tired or discouraged to get up some Sunday morning and go to church. He's the one who has been tempted in every way, just as we are, and so he understands.

This power to understand, to "sympathize with our weaknesses," is God's gift to us called *grace*. God gives this gift even if we don't deserve it. Grace is there for us; we can be confident of that fact. All we have to do is follow the directions and claim it for ourselves. As the Bible says in Hebrews 4:16, "Let us then approach the throne of grace with confidence, so that we may receive mercy and find grace to help us in our time of need."

DEVOTION

If you want to thrive, not just survive, in your college life, establish early on the habit of *devotion*—daily Bible reading and prayer. It won't be easy. Time is limited, and so many obligations will press in on you that it will be easy to let something as seemingly abstract as your daily devotions get lost in the crush.

Here are some ways to get started:

• *Establish a daily schedule that includes time for Bible reading and prayer.*

What's best for you? Early morning? Late evening just before you go to bed? A free period during the day when the dorm is empty?

• *Commit yourself to a faithful, daily period of devotion.*

Suppose the president of the United States were to invite you to breakfast each morning. Would you ignore the invitation or stand him up or arrive so late that you barely had time to be polite? Try treating your devotions as an appointment with God Almighty. It could change your attitude, help you think of devotions not as an obligation but as a privilege.

• *Select a quiet place where you can concentrate.*

While your dorm room is your only semi-private space, it may not be the best or only place for you to read and pray. Look around the dorm and the campus. Is the chapel open on your way to breakfast? Is there a carrel in the library you can use?

- *Try to follow a logical pattern in your reading.*

You don't read a novel by flipping here and there and reading a paragraph or a page at a time. Hit or miss doesn't work in Bible reading, either. If you need help to find a pattern and maintain a daily reading schedule, use one of the many prepared daily guides, some with notes and commentary, available from your church or bookstore.

- *Make a prayer list.*

All of us have wandering minds, especially when we try to pray. We need the help of a written list to keep before us the special needs for which we ought to pray—our own, our family's, and those of other loved ones—as well as larger issues. And don't forget to include thanksgiving for specific blessings.

- *Be as faithful as you can.*

If you miss a day or two, don't condemn yourself as a hypocrite; make sure to catch up the next day.

Think of your devotions as spiritual nourishment, comparable in some ways to physical nourishment. You couldn't thrive on one meal a week served on Sunday morning at 11:00 o'clock. You'd be famished by Monday night. Similarly, your spiritual hunger needs to be fed more than once a week.

Maybe you're enrolled in a Christian college that offers daily chapel services. These can be spiritually enriching, but they're not enough. You know that you can't develop a friendship or a romance in a crowd. You get to know someone well by spending time alone in conversation with that person, by intimately sharing each other's hopes and dreams. So, while getting to know God in community is important, it's also important to meet with him alone.

WORSHIP

When you first visited the campus and town, you may have checked to see what churches are in the community. Perhaps you've already decided to attend the worship services of the local congregation of your denomination. Or, if your denomination isn't represented in town, maybe you've chosen a similar form of worship with some other group. Or, even though there is a local church of your denomination, perhaps this is the time you've decided to investigate other churches and see how other Christians worship. Whatever you've decided, follow through.

Here are some ways to help make church-going a habit:

• *Plan ahead.*

Don't wait until Sunday morning to decide if or where you're going to church. Make church-going a part of your regular schedule, and plan your Saturday night and Sunday morning around that fact. If the church isn't within walking distance, know how you're going to get there. Many college-town churches arrange transportation for college students. (Some also offer college students Sunday dinner, either at church or in the homes of church families.)

• *Don't take forever to make up your mind about which church to attend.*

Some college freshmen have the best of intentions about selecting a church to attend, but they spend so many Sundays shopping around that the whole first semester is gone before they've finally settled in at one church.

Think of it this way: You don't really learn properly about history by randomly dropping in on one course here, a different course there. Sure, you can pick up some interesting information about the American Civil War in one class, the Roman Empire in another, the League of Nations in another; but such hit-or-miss shopping around gives you no way of arriving at any consistent understanding of historical developments and their interpretation.

It's much the same with church-hopping. You can't expect to grow in faith supported by the kind of biblical teaching you get from endlessly sampling the available churches and preachers. At some point, for the sake of spiritual nourishment, you need to commit yourself to a college-town "home church."

Of course, you can always decide to change your current church of preference and begin attending elsewhere. Or you can continue to attend the same church on Sunday mornings for continuity and for variety visit other congregations at other times: an Episcopal evensong on late Sunday afternoons or the Baptist church's evening service.

- *Understand why you go to church each Sunday.*

We go to church first of all to worship God. Not to meet other people or have a social hour or get all worked up about a political issue or even to find a safe haven from an unkind and godless roommate.

Worship means "worthiness," and we worship God because he is worthy of our praise. The focus of the time we spend in worship is honoring and adoring a holy God. That means offering praise and thanksgiving, song and prayer, being attentive to what God's Word and its teachings have to say, and being ready to act upon those teachings.

Second, we go to church to encourage each other in worship. Part of that encouragement is our very presence together, but another part is our financial support of the work of that church. Many college students act like freeloaders, never contributing a nickel toward the college-town church. You may not be able to give much, but try to give something.

• *Become involved.*

Once you've settled on a church away from home, take part as much as you reasonably can. If you can sing and have a couple of hours to rehearse every week or so, join the choir. If you can teach a Sunday school class faithfully, offer your talents. If you can be helpful as a volunteer in any capacity, make yourself useful.

• *Invite your roommate.*

Don't keep a good thing to yourself. You might be surprised at how many college students have never been to church because their families don't attend, and they've never known other people who go.

• *Recognize and appreciate the differences between a college-town church and your home church.*

When you go home for vacations, don't make unfair comparisons between churches. They probably serve two quite different congregations. Your college church may cater to a much younger group of people; its pastoral staff may be much more informal; its programs may seem more imaginative. But its membership will also be less permanent, because the mobile society of a college town comes and goes, and consequently you may not find the same kind of stability in the typical college-town congregation. So don't cut your ties with your home church. Some day, long after you're no longer a college student, you'll need what it or a church like it has to offer.

And what if you're enrolled at an evangelical college?

While some colleges make a point of expecting their students to worship at a local church, others waive such a rule. If your college leaves the decision to its students, be prepared for a shock: among college students at the most well-known Christian colleges, church attendance is often irregular at best. In fact, the standard joke at the cafeteria on Sundays has to do with attending various "churches of rest"—Pillow Presbyterian, Mattress Methodist, Bedside Baptist.

FELLOWSHIP

In addition to worship in your college-town church, you'll also find opportunities for fellowship—sharing your faith with friends at prayer meetings and Bible studies, at potluck suppers and picnics, at a Christmas caroling party or during a weekend at the beach. Whatever college or university you attend, the most encouraging part of your spiritual nurture will probably come from these experiences.

Often at a state university, you'll also find a row of houses representing various denominations, each house having a chaplain assigned to provide fellowship opportunities. You may even see a notice on your dorm bulletin board advertising a dorm fellowship group. At these same universities and colleges, you'll also find independent groups such as Inter-Varsity Christian Fellowship, Campus Crusade for Christ, the Fellowship of Christian Athletes, and the Navigators. We've given you the addresses of these groups in the next chapter.

At some universities these Christian groups may be struggling and need people like you to infuse them with fresh enthusiasm and energy. At other colleges, these groups are well established and attract large audiences at their weekly meetings. For instance, at the University of North Carolina, the three Lockerbies regularly attended the meetings of the Fellowship of

Christian Athletes with more than a hundred others—not all of whom, by the way, were necessarily varsity athletes. And Carolina's Inter-Varsity chapter was so large—over 800 members—that it divided into several smaller groups.

On an evangelical college campus, you'll find a different set of fellowship meetings, bringing together prayer and action groups supporting foreign missions, groups with specific vocational interests (such as nursing and elementary education), evangelistic teams, and musical ensembles. The efforts of these and other organizations will usually be coordinated by the college chaplain or pastor. Listen for announcements of these activities during your chapel services.

SERVICE

Worship and fellowship lead naturally to *service*, to the expression of your faith in acts of kindness toward others. Every college, including the most unreligious campus, offers some opportunities to serve others, whether as volunteers for urban relief work or as world hunger activists fasting to draw attention to the needs of others. As a Christian who cares for the needy, you can become involved.

But presumably you'll also find opportunities to serve through your college church or fellowship group. And if your group isn't actively serving others, why not suggest a program that reaches out to fulfill the command of the One who said, "I was hungry and you gave me something to eat, I was thirsty and you gave me something to drink, I was a stranger and you invited me in, I needed clothes and you clothed me, I was sick and you looked after me, I was in prison and you came and visited me. . . . I tell you the truth, whatever you did for one of the least of these brothers of mine, you did for me" (Matt. 25:35-40).

Devotion, worship, fellowship, and *service:* these are the means of grace that will never fail to support and encourage you in your time of need, whatever it may be.

A FINAL WORD

College is a time of preparation for the life and work to follow. If you've committed your life to love God and to serve him by serving others, your college years will be the time to find the particular sphere of service best suited to your gifts.

Each person has been given some kind of special potential to develop into a life's work. Yours may be a great singing voice or a talent for numbers; perhaps it's an ability to write clearly and powerfully or acute organizational skills; perhaps you can see through the fog of fancy language and interpret it simply for others, or maybe you have the gift of compassion and an unusual ability to comfort and console other people. Whether you become a singer or an accountant, an editor or a corporate executive, an attorney or a counselor, all your gifts must be identified, developed, polished, and offered to the world that needs what you have to offer.

You've started on the long road that will take you eventually to a life of service. Now high school, soon college—and afterward? Possibly graduate school or some other kind of professional training before you're established in your life's work.

You face important and challenging decisions. How wonderful to know that God takes a personal interest in each of those decisions, including your choice of college, your course of study, your life's companion, your field of service.

While you're preparing for what lies ahead, have a great time in college. If you're like most of us, you'll probably remember them as the best years of your life.

CHAPTER 11

Index of Resources

We've compiled a glossary, a bibliography, and a list of organizations to help you before and after you go to college. The glossary defines terms you'll hear in the college admissions and placement game as well on campus once you get there. The bibliography lists other references you might want to consult. And the organizational list gives the names and addresses of organizations you might want to ask for further information.

All terms that are cross-referenced appear in bold print.

GLOSSARY

academic adviser: Each new student will be assigned a faculty member to counsel him or her in freshman and sophomore course selection; subsequent advice usually comes from a **department adviser**.

accreditation: Before you apply to any college or university, you'll want to know that the institution can offer you a true education. Not every college does, and even those that may be strong in one department may be weak in the very area that most interests you. Look in the college's catalog or other promotional materials for its statement of accreditation. This means that the college has been examined by representatives of a regional organization—such as the Middle States Association of Colleges and Schools or the Southern Association of Colleges and Schools—and has been given a satisfactory evaluation. If an institution is not accredited, credits earned there may not transfer to another college, and it will be more difficult to enter graduate school. *Note:* There is no such thing as a national academic ranking of colleges. Such rankings do exist for football and basketball, but no college is "ranked number one in engineering" or "among the top ten in psychology" because there is no such official ranking; only the popular magazines and newspapers like *USA Today* offer any such supposed ranking. So beware of any college representative who makes such claims for his or her college.

achievement tests (ACH): See **College Board testing program.**

ACT: See **American College Test.**

Advanced Placement Program: See **College Board testing program.**

advanced standing: Status accorded students who have scored well on the College Board's Advanced Placement examinations. At the discretion of the individual college, a student may be exempted from taking introductory courses and/or given credit toward diploma requirements for work already completed in high school.

American College Test: A standardized admissions test of general aptitude used mainly by colleges in the West, Midwest, and Southwest. It's similar in purpose to the **SAT** but offers scores in English, mathematics, social studies, and the natural sciences. (The SAT offers only math and verbal scores.) The score range is 0 to 36; the average range of scores for college-bound students is 18 to 24. Some critics of the ACT claim that it's easier than the SAT and gives students who take it successfully an edge for getting into college, but we haven't found this to be true.

athletic scholarships. See **grant-in-aid.**

closed: Colleges permit each department to limit registration in every course, and sometimes the professor doesn't want more than 20 or 25 students in his class; sometimes the classroom seating limits the number of students. If you register late(r), a course you want may already be full and therefore "closed" to further registration unless one or more registered students drops the course. See **drop/add.**

College Board testing program: The College Entrance Examination Board (called the College Board for short) is an association of universities, colleges, and schools. It offers a variety of testing and evaluation programs for college admissions. These include the following:

Achievement Tests (ACH), administered in 16 subjects. Many colleges now require three ACH tests—usually those in English literature, English composition, and Mathematics I. It's also a good idea to take one test in what you think might be your **major.**

Advanced Placement Program (AP exams), involving a set of three-hour exams administered in most high-school subjects but demanding a demonstration of college-level knowledge and ability. Good scores may result in your college granting you **advanced standing**.

College Level Equivalency Program (CLEP), a series of standardized tests covering many subjects. These tests are intended for non-traditional college applicants—adults who have been out of school for a long time, individuals whose military service has delayed their entering college. The tests are offered as a means of validating life experience credit for **advanced standing**. They aren't a substitute for AP exams, although some community colleges and less academically competitive institutions may grant credit for good scores.

Preliminary Scholastic Aptitude Test (PSAT), a one-hour version of the **Scholastic Aptitude Test (SAT)**, which, in addition to offering practice for the SAT, also serves as the initial qualifying test for the **National Merit Scholarship Program.** Scores for each section (math and verbal) range from 20 to 80.

Scholastic Aptitude Test (SAT), a three-hour battery of tests divided into two basic sections: math (testing problem-solving and reasoning skills) and verbal (testing skills in vocabulary, reading comprehension, reasoning, and standard written English). Scores for each section range from 200 to 800; combined scores range from 400 to 1600. The average score among public high-school students is in the mid-400s for both the math and the verbal sections. The test developer for the College Board, **Educational Testing Service (ETS)**, claims that the SAT can be used to predict academic success or failure in college. It's widely used by colleges—especially the most selective—as an admissions screening device. In fact, despite what colleges themselves claim, its scores often serve as a final admissions standard for acceptance or rejection.

college fair: A gathering of college admissions officers and/or representatives in a single location (a school gym or community arena). Booths and exhibits display information about a variety of colleges to prospective applicants and their parents. A fair may include anywhere from 25 to 100 colleges. Obviously, it's a marketing device employed by the colleges, but it's also a good way to learn—superficially at least—about many colleges at once.

College Level Equivalency Program (CLEP): See College Board testing program.

college night: An event similar to the **college fair** but usually sponsored by the high school and conducted on a much smaller scale.

College Scholarship Service (CSS): An agency of the College Board which helps a student's family and his college to determine how much each can contribute to the costs of the student's education. To receive this service, the family must submit a **Financial Aid Form** and pay a modest fee.

common application: An application form used by many colleges. If you happen to be applying to several cooperating colleges, you may fill out one application, then make as many photocopies as you need. Colleges say a photocopy doesn't hurt your chances of being accepted. Your high school's official form and all your recommendations are a part of this common application, and you may also photocopy these.

comprehensive cost: The sum of all charges and expenses billed by a college for the academic year, including tuition, fees, room and board, books, and transportation.

cooperative education: Some colleges (for example, Northeastern University in Boston and Drexel University in Philadelphia) offer programs in which students divide their time between study on campus and work at study-related jobs. An accounting student may work in a bank; an English major may work in a publishing firm. Students receive academic credit as well as financial compensation for the work.

core curriculum: A varied selection of courses representing a sample of all areas of knowledge. Colleges that build on this core require all students to complete these courses, usually during their freshman and sophomore years. Students must complete most of these courses before they may go on to choose other courses or take only courses in their **major**.

co-requisite: A course that should be taken simultaneously with another designated course. See **prerequisite.**

course offerings: Subjects offered by each academic department during a semester or year. A student should consult each department in which he wishes to register for a course to determine if that particular course is being offered. Department decisions may supersede the college's published catalog.

credits: The system of measuring academic progress toward a diploma's minimum quota of 120 credits. Students who receive a passing grade are given credits for the number of hours spent in class each week: for instance, 3 hours in French class = 3 credits; 3 hours in biology class + 1 hour in biology lab = 4 credits. By accumulating hours each semester, a student accumulates sufficient credits to receive a degree.

cumulative GPA ("cume"): See **grade point average (GPA).**

dean's list: Most colleges recognize students who have a **cumulative GPA** of 3.0 or higher after three or four semesters and honor them by naming them to the dean's list, the roster of leading scholars.

deferred entrance: After being accepted for admission, a student may ask the college for a year's deferment. Given sufficient reasons for the request, most colleges will grant it, allowing the student to enroll the following year. Some colleges, however, will require re-application, and the student may risk being denied admission the second time around.

department adviser: When a student declares her **major** in a certain department, she is assigned to a professor—often a senior member of the faculty—in that department whose responsibility is to provide counsel on which courses the student should take to fulfill her academic needs and desires.

distributive requirement: This is similar to the requirement of a college with a **core curriculum,** except that the college doesn't specify which particular courses the student must take. Instead, it requires a student to choose his own courses from each division (the natural sciences, the social sciences, foreign languages, the humanities, the fine arts, and the performing arts), distributing his choices among departments.

drop/add: After a student registers for classes, he has a certain period of time in which to change courses by dropping out of one class and adding another, at no risk of incurring a failing grade (see **withdraw**). No record of the student's having enrolled in the dropped course appears on his transcript.

early acceptance: See **early decision.**

early action: See **early decision.**

early decision: A program offered by many colleges whereby a student applies by November 1 (November 15 in some instances) to one and only one college in order to get its decision by December 15. A few early-decision colleges may allow a student to apply to other schools that follow the regular application-admissions sequence and to wait until May 1 to make his final choice. Usually, however, the student must be committed to attending the early-decision college if he's accepted there, withdrawing all other applications. Sometimes a college rejects an applicant permanently in December; more often, an early-decision rejection still leaves the student a chance to be accepted later in the process. *Note:* Applying as an early-decision candidate to the most selective colleges helps only the very top students.

early notification: See **early decision.**

Educational Testing Service (ETS): The agency commissioned by the **College Board** to design, pre-test, refine, and administer all its admissions testing programs. While the College Board determines the purpose and nature of its tests, ETS is responsible for the exact content, mechanics, distribution, and scoring of the tests as well as the reporting of test scores.

Family Financial Statement (FFS): This statement is similar to the **Financial Aid Form** but related to the **American College Test** rather than the Scholastic Aptitude Test.

fees: Every college charges extra amounts to cover expenses related to student activities (student government, the student newspaper, social events, operating costs of the student union), athletic events (interscholastic events and intramural competition), laboratory fees (chemical use, breakage), musical events and instrument maintenance (concerts, piano tuning), and other hidden costs.

Financial Aid Form (FAF): An official document that the student who desires financial aid must have completed by her parents or whoever will be financially responsible for her college costs. The form requires them to provide federal income-tax information to show the family's financial resources. The completed form is sent along with a modest fee to the **College Scholarship Service (CSS)**. The CSS processes the form and sends the results to each college the student names. Those colleges that accept the student and wish to offer financial aid will use this information to determine how much the family can pay and how much aid the student needs. A new FAF must be filled out each year.

fraternities and sororities: Many traditional colleges and universities retain a nineteenth-century American custom of allowing secret societies with names consisting of Greek letters. These societies are national corporations whose local "chapters" are under the direct jurisdiction of the colleges. A student may join one of these societies for various reasons—the social life, the academic distinction, the social and community service the organization provides. A student who decides to join a fraternity or sorority must participate in a selection period called "rush," a hectic two weeks at the outset of the fall semester. Members of each chapter interview and critique prospective "pledges" before voting to accept or cut them. To become a pledge, a student may have to endure "hazing," a kind of ritual harassment. (This practice is declining, however, because it has sometimes led to tragedy.) Once accepted into the chapter, the new "brother" or "sister" may find living accommodations and meals in the "house" far more luxurious than those dorm life offered. But these improvements will also be more costly, and there will be obligations to the chapter: weekly meetings, service projects, and the responsibility to the national corporation of upholding its reputation. Joining a sorority or fraternity may be just right for some students; other students may find these groups snobbish, elitist, and even decadent.

grade point average (GPA): The academic average each semester or term computed by dividing the total number of quality points earned by the number of credits earned.

Quality points are assigned by multiplying the credits to be earned in any course (usually three) by the numerical value of the letter grade awarded. In most schools, A = 4.0, B = 3.0, C = 2.0, D = 1.0, F = O. So a three-credit course awarded a grade of B earns 9 quality points ($3 \times 3.0 = 9$). If a student taking four 3-hour courses receives A, B, C, and D in those courses, her GPA is computed as follows:

```
3 hours × 4.0 = 12.0
3 hours × 3.0 =  9.0
3 hours × 2.0 =  6.0
3 hours × 1.0 =  3.0
12 hours        30.0 = GPA of 2.5
```

Adding together every semester's GPA and dividing that total by the number of semesters completed adds up to a **cumulative GPA**, the average grade for all work completed.

grant: A financial aid award given to a student by the college. A grant may be an outright credit against **tuition**.

grant-in-aid: As explained in Chapter Five, pp. 67ff., all financial aid to athletes enrolled in NCAA-affiliated colleges and universities is strictly regulated. There is no such thing as an "athletic scholarship"; the correct term is "grant-in-aid." At every school each sport is assigned a maximum number of full grants. Football, for instance, may be allowed ninety grants; track and field, only twelve. Accordingly, a track coach must decide whether to offer twelve athletes a full grant or divide these allotted grants among eighteen or twenty team members. Every grant-in-aid specifies precisely what the recipient is being granted: for instance, one-half tuition or full tuition plus room allowance or full tuition plus room and board.

hook: Admissions slang meaning that an applicant who might not otherwise qualify for acceptance has some distinctive advantage that overcomes other liabilities. Having outstanding musical talent, belonging to a minority group, being the son or daughter of a distinguished alumnus—any of these could be the hook that gets a student into a school.

major: The course of study a student chooses as her primary academic focus. Most colleges expect a student to "declare" a major by the end of the sophomore year; that way she can spend her junior and senior years taking courses in the major, fulfilling the requirements of the department overseeing the major.

Many students change their minds after declaring their major. In some cases, this doesn't much matter; in other instances, switching majors is very complicated. An English major who decides to go pre-med and has no biology courses may find himself adding an extra year to his undergraduate career. A college often asks applicants to indicate their possible major. Answers aren't binding in any way; they're only a signal to the college that it may have to increase its faculty in certain departments.

minor: Most colleges encourage or permit a student to develop a second area of academic concentration called a minor. It involves taking about half as many courses as are being taken for the **major**. Frequently students minor in subject areas related to their majors, so a French major may minor in European history; a physics major may minor in mathematics or astronomy.

multiple applications: Some high-school seniors panic about getting into college, and in the belief that, by blanketing the field, they may guarantee at least one acceptance somewhere, they send out an inordinate number of applications. Several applications—three or four—are typical; multiple applications—say, sixteen—are foolish. Yet some students send many more than that. If students are properly guided in their college choices, it is absolutely unnecessary for them to apply to more than four or five colleges.

multiple deposits: A student accepted at more than one college may decide to send the required deposits (each ranging from $200 to $500) which guarantee that a place will be held for him at each school. This is a kind of insurance policy that allows the student some extra time in which to make a final decision. (Once the student chooses one college and notifies the others that he won't be attending there, he shouldn't expect or ask to get the deposits back.) While this practice may be frowned upon by admissions officers and high-school counselors, it happens all the time, because most students would rather be safe than sorry.

National Merit Scholarship Program: A major four-year scholarship is awarded to the top one to two percent of qualified high-school graduates. To be eligible, a student must take the **PSAT** no later than the fall of her junior year. Each state determines its own index of eligibility, so that a high score in a highly competitive state might not qualify a student for final selection, even though the same score might win a scholarship for a student in a less competitive state.

NCAA Proposition 48: The National Collegiate Athletic Association governs athletic competition at most major colleges and universities. Two of its three divisions, I and II, may offer grants to students recruited to participate in athletics; however, the institutions that recruit them must abide by strict recruiting regulations. One of these pertains to high-school academic performance as gauged by both **grade point average** and scores from either the **Scholastic Aptitude Test** or the **American College Test**. To be eligible for a grant, a high-school prospect must attain a 2.0 (C) average in 11 core courses, plus an SAT score of 700 out of 1600 or an ACT score of 15 out of 36. For further information, write or call the NCAA: Nall Avenue at 63rd Street, P.O. Box 1906, Mission, KS 66201, ph. 913-384-3220.

open admissions: The policy of accepting for admission all students who apply. Usually this policy relates to high-school graduates applying to their own state university or to state-sponsored community colleges. The more selective colleges don't practice open admissions.

pass/fail: Some departments or professors may offer students an alternative to being given grades of A, B, C, D, or F—being rated according to the pass/fail system. A student carrying a particularly heavy course load may wish to enjoy a certain professor's class without worrying about having to get a B to remain on the **dean's list**, so he chooses the pass/fail grading option. But he must make his choice at the beginning of the semester, and he can't change it later.

Pell Grant: Named for Rhode Island Senator Claiborne Pell, this federal grant (formerly known as the Basic Education Opportunity Grant) is based solely on financial need. The **Financial Aid Form** contains a question asking if you wish to be considered for a Pell Grant. If you fill out this form, check "Yes," even if you don't think your chances of getting a grant are very good. You might be pleasantly surprised.

Perkins Loan Program (formerly **National Direct Student Loan [NDSL]**): Federal loans distributed through college channels rather than banks. They offer even lower interest rates than the **Stafford Loan**, but their availability is more limited, because a college's own funds are involved, whereas a Stafford Loan involves bank funds. The repayment plan is the same as that of the Stafford Loan: repayment can begin several months after graduation, and the borrower can take up to ten years to pay off the loan.

Preliminary Scholastic Aptitude Test (PSAT): See **College Board testing program.**

pre-registration: The time designated for students already in school to select courses for the following semester before new students are eligible to register. This process allows a college to plan according to student interest and curriculum needs.

prerequisite: A course required in order to take a subsequent course. Prerequisite courses provide basic background for more advanced courses.

quality points: See **grade point average.**

reply date: Every college offering admission to a student specifies a date by which she must accept or decline the offer. In the normal admissions process, this date is usually May 1. "Early decision" colleges will specify an earlier reply date. *Note:* The sooner you reply, the better, since financial aid and housing information will be sent only after you have confirmed your acceptance, and the earlier you get these wheels in motion, the better the deal you'll probably get.

Reserve Officers Training Corps (ROTC): A program of military training sponsored by the U.S. Army, Navy, and Air Force whereby students may be commissioned as officers upon graduation. ROTC candidates receive stipends toward their college expenses but must commit themselves to a period of active service following college, after which they must maintain continuing reserve status. Special ROTC scholarships are also available to highly qualified candidates.

"rocks for jocks": An uncomplimentary reference to an easy course (e.g., "Geology for Athletes") available in some colleges as a **slide** to keep inferior students eligible for athletic competition.

rolling admissions: An admissions process that has no set deadline for applications but simply rolls along until the student body is complete. Such colleges act promptly on applications; students can usually receive notification within a few weeks of mailing their applications. This procedure is often used by colleges experiencing difficulty in attracting applicants.

room and board: The cost of a student's college-provided dormitory accommodations and meals in the college cafeteria.

scholarship: A designated sum of money, often obtained as earnings from an investment or endowment and named for its donor, that is made available by a college, company, or foundation to qualified candidates. The provider designates the recipients of each scholarship. Scholarships may be awarded for any reason—personal character, leadership qualities, high academic potential, musical talent, and so on—except athletic ability. Under NCAA regulations, all athletes receiving financial aid must not exceed the limitations of a stipulated grant. In other words, no athlete can receive a scholarship in addition to an NCAA grant-in-aid.

Scholastic Aptitude Test (SAT): See **College Board testing program.**

slide: A course well known to be extremely easy. It involves few assignments and no homework, and minimal attendance is required.

Stafford Loan (formerly called **GSL**): A federal program channeled through local banks and savings institutions whereby a student or his parents may borrow up to $2500 per year (as of 1990) at a rate much lower than the standard interest rate. The borrower doesn't need to begin repaying the loan until several months after the student graduates from college or graduate school; thereafter, the borrower has ten years to pay off the loan.

Supplemental Education Opportunity Grant (SEOG): A federal financial-aid program for exceptionally needy students, offering supplemental aid to the **Pell Grant**.

Test of English as a Foreign Language (TOEFL): A test offered to students whose native language is not English. Such students usually score poorly on the **Scholastic Aptitude Test** or the **American College Test** but can do much better on the TOEFL. A good TOEFL score can help get a student into college since it compensates in some ways for poor scores on the verbal part of the SAT or the ACT.

transcript: Every academic institution, from elementary school to post-graduate school, keeps records of every student's achievement: the period of enrollment, the courses taken, the grades received, the diploma or degree granted, and other pertinent information on academic status. This record is transcribed to a formal document—thus called a transcript—bearing the seal of the school or college. A student's transcript is personal and highly confidential, but it is also the property of the school or college and may not be altered or tampered with. Copies of a student's high-school transcript will be sent, upon request, anywhere he applies for freshman admission or, later, for **transfer**.

transfer: After a semester or more, a student may decide that the college she chose doesn't offer exactly what she needs, so she may want to leave and enroll somewhere else. Since she wants to receive credit for the courses she's already taken, she must apply for admission as a transfer student, requesting full recognition of her present academic standing. If her grades are good (and her college is accredited), she probably won't have any trouble transferring all or most of her already earned credits to her new college. But every student considering a transfer should read the fine print in the new college's catalog: it may have a core of required courses every student, including transfers, must complete, and a decision to transfer there could extend studies by a year or more.

tuition: The price tag a college puts on its instruction; what a student must pay for the privilege of learning from its professors and using its resources.

wait list: If a college doesn't immediately accept a student but wishes to keep him interested, it may choose to assign him to its wait list. If openings occur because some of those applicants who've been accepted decide not to enroll, the college then accepts names from its wait list.

If you end up on a wait list for your first-choice college and are accepted by your alternate, try this strategy: notify the college that's wait-listed you that you want to remain on the list, but at the same time send the deposit to your alternate. Then, if you don't make it off the wait list at your first choice, you can take up the offer of your alternate.

withdraw: As part of its academic calendar, every college establishes its time limit for both the **drop/add** option and the withdrawal option. This second option gives the student a chance to try a course to see whether or not it satisfies her, then to withdraw if it doesn't. If a student has been keeping up with the course work and decides to withdraw within the stipulated time limit (usually within four weeks of the beginning of a semester), she can do so without penalty. Her **transcript** will bear the notation "withdrawn passing." But if she decides to leave the course after the stipulated time limit, the transcript note reads "withdrawn failing" because she hasn't completed the course's demands.

work-study program: A program jointly sponsored by the federal government and a college that offers a student part-time employment. Federal funds help to subsidize the wages paid by the college. A student may use his earnings in any way he wishes, but the clear understanding is that this money helps to pay for his college expenses.

BIBLIOGRAPHY

The following college guides provide background information and, in some instances, comparisons of various schools. You'll find most of these in your high-school counselor's office, in your local public library, or in bookstores.

Barron's In-Depth Profiles of American Colleges (Barron's Educational Series)
Barron's Profiles of American Colleges (Barron's Educational Series)
The College Handbook (College Board)
Comparative Guide to American Colleges, Cass and Birnbaum (Harper & Row)
Guide to Alternative Colleges and Universities
Index of Majors (College Board)
Insider's Guide to College (Yale Daily News)
Lovejoy's Concise College Guide, Straughn and Straughn (Monarch Press)
Peterson's Annual Guide to Undergraduate Study (Peterson's Guides)
Peterson's Consider a Christian College (Peterson's Guides)

The following books offer additional information on admissions and financial aid:

Betterton, Don M. *How to Pay for College* (Peterson's Guides)
Cassidy, Daniel, and Michael Alves. *The Scholarship Book: The Complete Guide to Private-Sector Scholarships, Grants, and Loans for Undergraduates* (Prentice-Hall)
The College Board. *The College Cost Book* (College Board)
Holmes, Max. *Clear and Simple Guide to Writing Your College Application and Essay* (Monarch Press)
Hoy, John C. *Choosing a College*

Kennedy, Joyce L., et al. *The College Financial Aid Emergency Kit* (Sun Features)

Krefetz, Gerald. *How to Pay for Your Children's College Education* (College Board)

Moll, Richard W. *Playing the Private College Admissions Game* (Penguin Books)

Nemko, Martin. *How to Get an Ivy League Education at a State University* (Avon Books)

Ripple, Gary G. *Do It—Write: How to Prepare a Great College Application* (Octameron Assocs.)

————. *Campus Pursuit: How to Make the Most of the College Visit and Interview* (Octameron Assocs.)

Wall, Edward B. *Behind the Scenes: An Inside Look at the Selective College Admission Process* (Octameron Assocs.)

———

For computer software assistance, consider these:

The College Board's College Explorer (IBM #003195; Apple #003187), available from College Board Publications, Department N06, Box 886, New York, NY 10101

The College Board's College Entry (IBM #003233; Apple II #003241), available from same address as above)

Peterson's College Selection Service (IBM PC #8993; Apple II #8934), available from Peterson's Guides, P.O. Box 2123, Princeton, NJ 08543

The following (books unless otherwise specified) offer helpful advice about facing particular problems:

Depression

Beck, A. T. *Depression* (Harper & Row)
Depression: Recognizing It and Treating It (slide-tape presentation available through IBIS Media)
Grinker, R. R., et al. *The Phenomenon of Depression* (Hoeber)
Kraines, Samuel, et al. *Help for the Depressed* (C. C. Thomas)
Phillips, Beeman. *School Stress and Anxiety* (Human Sciences Press)

Suicide

Berman, A. L. *The Problem of Teenage Suicide* (American Psychological Association)
Hafen, B. Q., and Frandsen, K. J. *Youth Suicide: Depression and Loneliness* (EvergreenPublishing Co.)
Joan, Polly. *Preventing Teenage Suicide* (Human Sciences Press)
Shneidman, E. S., ed. *Death and the College Student* (Human Sciences Press)

Alcoholism

Cohen, Susan, and Daniel Cohen. *A Six-Pack and a Fake I.D.* (M. Evans)
Langone, John B. *Bombed, Buzzed, Smashed, or . . . Sober: A Book about Alcohol* (Little, Brown)
Newman, Susan. *You Can Say No to a Drink or a Drug* (Perigee Books)

Woititz, J. G. *Adult Children of Alcoholics* (Health Communications)
———. *Struggle for Intimacy* (Health Communications)

Substance Abuse

Brown, David. *Crack and Cocaine* (Gloucester Press)
Cohen, Miriam. *Marijuana: Its Effects on Mind and Body* (Chelsea House)
Dying to Do Drugs (Christopher News Notes, New York)
Glassner, Barry, and Julia Loughlin. *Drugs in Adolescent Worlds: Burnouts to Straights* (St. Martin's Press)
Hulburd, David. *H Is for Heroin* (Doubleday)
Nahas, Gabriel. *Marijuana: The Deceptive Weed* (Raven Press)
———. *Keep Off the Grass* (Paul Eriksson)
Woods, Geraldine. *Drug Use and Drug Abuse* (Franklin Watts)

Eating Disorders

Boskind-White, Marlene, and White, William. *Bulimarexia: The Binge-Purge Cycle* (W. W. Norton)
Brumberg, Joan Jacobs. *Fasting Girls: The Emergence of Anorexia Nervosa as a Modern Disease* (Harvard University Press)
Byrne, Katherine. *A Parent's Guide to Anorexia and Bulimia* (Schocken Books)
Landau, Elaine. *Why Are They Starving Themselves? Understanding Anorexia and Bulimia* (Julian Messner)
Levenkron, Steven. *Treating and Overcoming Anorexia Nervosa* (Warner Books)
MacLeod, Sheila. *The Art of Starvation* (Schocken Books)
Rumney, Avis. *Dying to Please: Anorexia Nervosa and Its Cure* (McFarland & Co.)

Sexual Relations and Sexually Transmitted Diseases

Alcorn, Randy. *Christians in the Wake of the Sexual Revolution: Recovering Our Sexual Sanity* (Multnomah Press)

Huggett, Joyce. *Dating, Sex and Friendship: An Open and Honest Guide to Healthy Relationships* (Inter-Varsity Press)

Koop, C. Everett. *AIDS: Everything You and Your Family Need to Know* (videotape available from Home Box Office, Inc.)

Short, Ray E. *Sex, Love, or Infatuation: How Can I Really Know?* (Augsburg)

Trager, Oliver, ed. *AIDS: Plague or Panic?* (Facts on File)

White, John. *Eros Defiled: The Christian and Sexual Sin* (Inter-Varsity Press)

The following books deal with general concerns important to college students and their parents:

Coopersmith, Stanley, ed. *The Antecedents of Self-Esteem* (Consulting Psychologists Press)

Gerl, George, and George Lane. *Two Called Together: A Marriage Workbook* (Loyola University Press)

Hawley, Richard A. *The Big Issues in the Adolescent Journey* (Walker & Co.)

Lewis, C. S. *Mere Christianity* (Macmillan)

Lockerbie, D. Bruce. *Thinking and Acting like a Christian* (Multnomah Press)

ORGANIZATIONS TO CONSULT

The following organizations can be helpful in providing information about their group meetings on various campuses:

Campus Crusade for Christ
Arrowhead Springs
San Bernardino, CA 92414

Fellowship of Christian Athletes
8701 Leeds Road
Kansas City, MO 64129

Inter-Varsity Christian Fellowship
233 Langdon
Madison, WI 53703

The Navigators
P.O. Box 6000
Colorado Springs, CO 80934